POEMS
AND
PROBLEMS

VLADIMIR NABOKOV

POEMS AND PROBLEMS

McGraw-Hill Book Company

New York   St. Louis   San Francisco   Bogotá   Guatemala
Hamburg   Lisbon   Madrid   Mexico   Montreal
Panama   Paris   San Juan   São Paulo   Tokyo   Toronto

POEMS AND PROBLEMS

Copyright © 1970 by McGraw-Hill International,
Inc. All rights reserved. Printed in the United States
of America. No part of this publication may be
reproduced, stored in a retrieval system, or
transmitted, in any form or by any means, electronic,
mechanical, photocopying, recording, or otherwise,
without the prior permission of McGraw-Hill, Inc.

1234567890 FGFG 87654321

Library of Congress Cataloging in Publication Data

Nabokov, Vladimir Vladimirovich, 1899–1977.
   Poems and problems.

   (McGraw-Hill paperbacks)
   Bibliography: p.
   Contents: Thirty-nine Russian poems [with English
translations]—Fourteen English poems—Eighteen chess
problems—Solutions.
   I. Title.
[PG3476.N3A17 1981]   891.71′42   81–8325
ISBN 0-07-045726-3 (pbk.)   AACR2

First paperback edition, 1981.

To Véra

CONTENTS

INTRODUCTION

This volume consists of three sections: a batch of thirty-nine Russian poems, given in the original and in translation; fourteen poems which I wrote directly in English after 1940 (the year of my leaving Europe for the United States); and eighteen chess problems.

The Russian poems represent only a small fraction—hardly more than one percent—of the steady mass of verse which I began to exude in my early youth, more than half a century ago, and continued to do so, with monstrous regularity, especially during the twenties and thirties, then petering out in the next two decades, when a meager output of a score or so hardly exceeded the number of poems I wrote in English.

What can be called rather grandly my European period of versemaking seems to show several distinctive stages: an initial one of passionate and commonplace love verse (not represented in this edition); a period reflecting utter distrust of the so-called October Revolution; a period (reaching well into the 1920s) of a kind of private curatorship, aimed at preserving nostalgic retrospections and developing Byzantine imagery (this has been mistaken by some readers for an interest in "religion," which, beyond literary stylization, never meant anything to me); a period lasting another decade or so during which I set myself to illustrate the principle of making a short poem contain a plot and tell a story (this in a way expressed my impatience with the dreary drone of the anemic "Paris school" of émigré poetry); and finally, in the late thirties, and especially in the following decades, a sudden liberation from self-imposed shackles, resulting both in a sparser output and in a belatedly discovered robust style. Selecting poems for this volume proved less difficult than translating them.

For the last ten years, I have been promoting, on every possible occasion, literality, i.e., rigid fidelity, in the translation of Russian verse. Treating a text in that way is an honest and delightful procedure, when the text is a recognized masterpiece, whose every detail must be faithfully rendered in English. But what about faithfully englishing one's own verse, written half a century or a quarter of a century ago? One has to fight a vague embarrassment; one cannot help squirming and wincing; one feels rather like a potentate swearing allegiance to his own self or a conscientious priest blessing his own bathwater. On the other hand, if one contemplates, for one wild moment, the possibility of paraphrasing and improving one's old verse, a horrid sense of falsification makes one scamper back and cling like a baby ape to rugged fidelity. There is only one little compromise I have accepted: whenever possible, I have welcomed rhyme, or its shadow; but I have never twisted the tail of a line for the sake of consonance; and the original measure has not been kept if readjustments of sense had to be made for its sake.

There is not much to say about the section of fourteen English poems, all written in America and all published in *The New Yorker*. Somehow, they are of a lighter texture than the Russian stuff, owing, no doubt, to their lacking that inner verbal association with old perplexities and constant worry of thought which marks poems written in one's mother tongue, with exile keeping up its parallel murmur and a never-resolved childhood plucking at one's rustiest chords.

Finally, there is the chess. I refuse to apologize for its inclusion. Chess problems demand from the composer the same virtues that characterize all worthwhile art: originality, invention, conciseness, harmony, complexity, and splendid insincerity. The composing of those ivory-and-ebony riddles is a comparatively rare gift and an extravagantly sterile occupation; but then all art is inutile, and divinely so, if compared to a number of more popular human endeavors. Problems are the poetry of chess, and its poetry, as all poetry, is subject to changing trends with various conflicts between old and new schools. Modern conventionalism repels me in chess problems as much as it does in "social realism" or "abstract" sculpture. More specifically speaking, I detest so-called "task" problems (mechanically committed to achieve a Stakhanovist maximum of related patterns), and I strictly avoid postkey duals (another Soviet fashion), even when they come after nonthematic Black moves.

I started to devise chess problems in late 1917, a date easy to remember. Many of my oldest compositions have survived in bedraggled notebooks—and seem today even worse than the elegies in my young script which they face. As I look through later unpublished jottings, those of my Cambridge University years and those of my Berlin stage, I find nothing worth printing today. The chess manuscripts of the first twenty years of my American period have been mislaid, and I am unable to reconstitute those compositions, though I still remember some of them in blurred outline. Their loss does not matter. The present collection of a few problems composed recently forms an adequate corollary to my later verse.

Montreux   Vladimir Nabokov
December, 1969

THIRTY-NINE
RUSSIAN
POEMS

1
ДОЖДЬ ПРОЛЕТЕЛ

Дождь пролетел и сгорел налету.
  Иду по румяной дорожке.
Иволги свищут, рябины в цвету,
4   Белеют на ивах сережки.

Воздух живителен, влажен, душист.
  Как жимолость благоухает!
Кончиком вниз наклоняется лист
8   И с кончика жемчуг роняет.

Выра, 1917 г.

1

The Rain Has Flown

The rain has flown and burnt up in flight.
　　I tread the red sand of a path.
Golden orioles whistle, the rowan is in bloom,
4　　the catkins on sallows are white.

The air is refreshing, humid and sweet.
　　How good the caprifole smells!
Downward a leaf inclines its tip
8　　and drops from its tip a pearl.

Vyra, 1917

Note

1/ *Dozhd' proletel* The phrase *letit dozhd'*, "rain is flying," was borrowed by the author from an old gardener (described in *Speak, Memory*, Chapter Two *et passim*) who applied it to light rain soon followed by sunshine. The poem was composed in the park of our country place in the last spring my family was to spend there. It was first published in *Dva Puti*, a collection of juvenile poems (a schoolmate's and mine), in Petrograd, January 1918, and was set to music by the composer Vladimir Ivanovich Pohl at Yalta, early 1919.

2
К СВОБОДЕ

Ты медленно бредешь по улицам бессонным;
на горестном челе нет прежнего луча,
зовущего к любви и высям озаренным.
В одной руке дрожит потухшая свеча.
Крыло подбитое по трупам волоча
и заслоняя взор локтем окровавленным,
обманутая вновь, ты вновь уходишь прочь,
а за тобой, увы, стоит все та же ночь!

Крым, 1917

2
To Liberty

Slowly you wander through the sleepless streets.
From your sad brow gone is the former ray,
that called us toward love and shining heights.

4   Your trembling hand holds an extinguished taper.
Dragging your broken wing over dead men,
your bloodstained elbow covering your eyes,
once more deceived, you once again depart,

8   and the old night, alas, remains behind.

Crimea, 1917

Note

The main—and, indeed, only—interest of these lines resides in their revealing the disappointment of the intelligentsia, who had welcomed the liberal Revolution of the spring of 1917 and was distressed by the Bolshevist reactionary insurrection in the autumn of the same year. The fact of that reactionary regime having now survived for more than half a century adds a prophetic touch to a young poet's conventional poem. It may have been published in 1918, in some Yalta newspaper, but was not included in any of my later collections.

3
ЕЩЕ БЕЗМОЛВСТВУЮ

Еще безмолвствую и крепну я в тиши.
Созданий будущих заоблачные грани
еще скрываются во мгле моей души,
как выси горные в предутреннем тумане.

Приветствую тебя, мой неизбежный день!
Все шире, шире даль, светлей, разнообразней,
и на звенящую, на первую ступень
всхожу, исполненный блаженства и боязни.

Крым, 1919 г.

3
I Still Keep Mute

I still keep mute—and in the hush grow strong.
The far-off crests of future works, amidst
the shadows of my soul are still concealed
4   like mountaintops in pre-auroral mist.

I greet you, my inevitable day!
The skyline's width, variety and light
increase; and on the first, resounding step
8   I go up, filled with terror and delight.

Crimea, 1919

4

НОМЕР В ГОСТИНИЦЕ

Не то кровать, не то скамья.
Угрюмо-желтые обои.
Два стула. Зеркало кривое.
4   Мы входим — я и тень моя.

Окно со звоном открываем:
спадает отблеск до земли.
Ночь бездыханна. Псы вдали
8   тишь рассекают пестрым лаем.

Я замираю у окна,
и в черной чаше небосвода,
как золотая капля меда,
12   сверкает сладостно луна.

Севастополь, 1919 г.

4
Hotel Room

Not quite a bed, not quite a bench.
Wallpaper: a grim yellow.
A pair of chairs. A squinty looking-glass.
4   We enter—my shadow and I.

We open with a vibrant sound the window:
the light's reflection slides down to the ground.
The night is breathless. Distant dogs
8   with varied barks fracture the stillness.

Stirless, I stand there at the window,
and in the black bowl of the sky
glows like a golden drop of honey
12   the mellow moon.

Sebastopol, 1919

5
ПРОВАНС

Слоняюсь переулками без цели,
прислушиваюсь к древним временам:
при Цезаре цикады те же пели,
и то же солнце сткалось по стенам.

Поет платан, и ствол — в пятнистом блеске;
поет лавченка; можно отстранить
легко звенящий бисер занавески:
поет портной, вытягивая нить.

И женщина у круглого фонтана
поет, полощет синее белье,
и пятнами ложится тень платана
на камни, на корзину, на нее.

Как хорошо в звенящем мире этом
скользить плечом вдоль меловых оград,
быть русским заблудившимся поэтом
средь лепета латинского цикад!

Солльес Пон, 1923 г.

5
Provence

I wander aimlessly from lane to lane,
bending a careful ear to ancient times:
the same cicadas sang in Caesar's reign,
4   upon the walls the same sun clings and climbs.

The plane tree sings: with light its trunk is pied;
the little shop sings: delicately tings
the bead-stringed curtain that you push aside—
8   and, pulling on his thread, the tailor sings.

And at a fountain with a rounded rim,
rinsing blue linen, sings a village girl,
and mottle shadows of the plane tree swim
12   over the stone, the wickerwork, and her.

What bliss it is, in this world full of song,
to brush against the chalk of walls, what bliss
to be a Russian poet lost among
16   cicadas trilling with a Latin lisp!

Solliès-Pont, 1923

6

LA BONNE LORRAINE

Жгли англичане, жгли мою подругу,
на площади в Руане жгли ее.
Палач мне продал черную кольчугу,
4   клювастый шлем и мертвое копье.

Ты здесь со мной, железная святая,
и мир с тех пор стал холоден и прост:
косая тень и лестница витая,
8   и в бархат ночи вбиты гвозди звезд.

Моя свеча над ржавою резьбою
дрожит и каплет воском на ремни.
Мы, воины, летали за тобою,
12   в твои цвета окрашивая дни.

Но опускала ночь свое забрало,
и молча выскользнув из лат мужских,
ты, белая и слабая, сгорала
16   в объятьях верных рыцарей твоих.

Берлин, 1924 г.

6
La Bonne Lorraine

The English burned her, burned my girl,
burned her in Rouen's market square.
The deathsman sold me a black coat of mail,
4   a beaked helmet and a dead spear.

You are here with me, iron saint,
and the world has grown cold and stark:
slanting shadows, and winding stairs,
8   and the night's velvet nailed with stars.

Above rusty traceries, my candle
flickers and drops wax on the straps.
We, warriors, flew in your wake
12   and tinctured our days in your colors.

But when night lowered its vizor,
in silence you slipped out of masculine armor,
and white and weak you would burn
16   in the embrace of your faithful knights.

Berlin, 1924

7

ГЕРБ

Лишь отошла земля родная,
в соленой тьме дохнул нордост,
как меч алмазный обнажая
средь облаков стремнину звезд.

Мою тоску, воспоминанья
клянусь я царственно беречь,
с тех пор как принял герб изгнанья:
на черном поле звездный меч.

Берлин, 1925 г.

7
The Blazon

As soon as my native land had receded
in the briny dark the northeaster struck,
like a sword of diamond revealing
among the clouds a chasm of stars.

My yearning ache, my recollections
I swear to preserve with royal care
ever since I adopted the blazon of exile:
on a field of sable a starry sword.

4

8

Berlin, 1925

8
МАТЬ

Смеркается. Казнен. С Голгофы отвалив,
спускается толпа, виясь между олив,
   подобно медленному змию;
и матери глядят, как под гору, в туман,
увещевающий уводит Иоанн
   седую, страшную Марию.

Уложит спать ее, и сам приляжет он,
и будет до утра подслушивать сквозь сон
   ее рыданья и томленье.
Что если у нее остался бы Христос,
и плотничал, и пел? Что если этих слез
   не стоит наше искупленье?

Воскреснет Божий Сын, сияньем окружен;
у гроба, в третий день, виденье встретит жен,
   вотще купивших ароматы;
светящуюся плоть ощупает Фома;
от веянья чудес земля сойдет с ума,
   и будут многие распяты.

Мария, что тебе до бреда рыбарей?
Неосязаемо над горестью твоей
   дни проплывают, и ни в третий,
ни в сотый, никогда не вспрянет он на зов,
твой смуглый первенец, лепивший воробьев
   на солнцепеке, в Назарете.

Берлин, 1925

8
The Mother

Night falls. He has been executed.
From Golgotha the crowd descends and winds
between the olive trees, like a slow serpent;
and mothers watch as John downhill
into the mist, with urgent words, escorts
6   gray, haggard Mary.

To bed he'll help her, and lie down himself,
and through his slumber hear till morning
   her tossings and her sobs.
What if her son had stayed at home with her,
and carpentered and sung? What if those tears
12   cost more than our redemption?

The Son of God will rise, in radiance orbed;
on the third day a vision at the tomb
will meet the wives who bought the useless myrrh;
Thomas will feel the luminescent flesh;
the wind of miracles will drive men mad,
18   and many will be crucified.

Mary, what are to you the fantasies
of fishermen? Over your grief days skim
   insensibly, and neither on the third
nor hundredth, never will he heed your call
and rise, your brown firstborn who baked mud
     sparrows
24   in the hot sun, at Nazareth.

Berlin, 1925

9

ЛЮБЛЮ Я ГОРУ

Люблю я гору в шубе черной
лесов еловых, потому
что в темноте чужбины горной
я ближе к дому моему.

4

Как не узнать той хвои плотной
и как с ума мне не сойти
хотя б от ягоды болотной,
заголубевшей на пути?

8

Чем выше темные, сырые
тропинки вьются, тем ясней
приметы с детства дорогие
равнины северной моей.

12

Не так ли мы по склонам рая
взбираться будем в смертный час,
все то любимое встречая,
что в жизни возвышало нас?

16

Фельдберг, 1925 г.

9
I Like That Mountain

I like that mountain in its black pelisse
of fir forests—because
in the gloom of a strange mountain country
I am closer to home.

How should I not know those dense needles,
and how should I not lose my mind
at the mere sight of that peatbog berry
showing blue along my way?

The higher the dark and damp
trails twist upward, the clearer
grow the tokens, treasured since childhood,
of my northern plain.

Shall we not climb thus
the slopes of paradise, at the hour of death,
meeting all the loved things
that in life elevated us?

Feldberg, 1925

10
СНОВИДЕНИЕ

Будильнику на утро задаю
        урок, и в сумрак отпускаю,
как шар воздушный, комнату мою,
4   и облегченно в сон вступаю.

Меня берет, уже во сне самом,
        как бы вторичная дремота.
Туманный стол. Сидящих за столом
8   не вижу. Все мы ждем кого-то.

Фонарь карманный кто-то из гостей
        на дверь как пистолет наводит,
и ростом выше и лицом светлей,
12   убитый друг со смехом входит.

Я говорю без удивленья с ним,
        живым, и знаю, нет обмана.
Со лба его сошла, как легкий грим,
16   смертельная когда-то рана.

Мы говорим. Мне весело. Но вдруг —
        заминка, странное стесненье.
Меня отводит в сторону мой друг
20   и что-то шепчет в объясненье.

Но я не слышу. Длительный звонок
        на представленье созывает:
будильник повторяет свой урок,
24   и день мне веки прорывает.

Лишь миг один неправильный на вид,
        мир падает, как кошка, сразу

10
The Dream

To my alarm clock its lesson I set
for next morning, and into the darkness
I release my bedroom like a balloon,
4   and step into sleep with relief.

Then, in sleep itself, I'm possessed by a sort
of subordinate drowsiness. Dimly
I see a round table. I cannot make out
8   those sitting at it. We're all waiting for somebody.

One of the guests has a pocket flashlight
that he trains on the door, like a pistol;
and higher in stature, and brighter in face
12   a dead friend of mine enters, laughing.

Without any astonishment I talk to him,
now alive, and I feel there is no deception.
The once mortal wound has gone from his brow
16   as if it had been some light make-up.

We talk, I feel gay. Then, suddenly,
there's a falter, an odd embarrassment.
My friend leads me aside
20   and whispers something in explanation.

But I do not hear. A long-ringing bell
summons to the performance:
the alarm clock repeats its lesson
24   and daylight breaks through my eyelids.

Looking, just for one moment, of the wrong shape,
the world lands catlike, on all

на все четыре лапы, и стоит,
28   знакомый разуму и глазу.

Но, Боже мой, когда припомнишь сон,
      случайно днем в чужой гостиной,
или, сверкнув, придет на память он
32   пред оружейною витриной,

как благодарен силам неземным,
      что могут мертвые нам сниться,
как этим сном, событием ночным,
36   душа смятенная гордится!

Берлин, 1927 г.

its four feet at once, and now stands
28   familiar both to the mind and the eye.

But, good Lord—when by chance the dream is
      recalled
during the day, in somebody's drawing room,
or when in a flash it comes back to one
32   in front of a gunsmith's window—

how grateful one is to unearthly powers
that the dead can appear in one's sleep,
how proud of the dream, of that nighttime event,
36   is one's shaken soul!

Berlin, 1927

11
СНИМОК

На пляже в полдень лиловатый,
в морском каникульном раю,
снимал купальщик полосатый
свою счастливую семью.

И замирает мальчик голый,
и улыбается жена,
в горячий свет, в песок веселый,
как в серебро погружена.

И полосатым человеком
направлен в солнечный песок,
мигнул и щелкнул черным веком
фотографический глазок.

Запечатлела эта пленка
все, что могла она поймать:
оцепеневшего ребенка,
его сияющую мать,

и ведерцо, и две лопаты,
и в стороне песчаный скат.
И я, случайный соглядатай,
на заднем плане тоже снят.

Зимой, в неведомом мне доме
покажут бабушке альбом,
и будет снимок в том альбоме,
и буду я на снимке том:

11
The Snapshot

Upon the beach at violet-blue noon,
in a vacational Elysium
a striped bather took
4   a picture of his happy family.

And very still stood his small naked boy,
and his wife smiled,
in ardent light, in sandy bliss
8   plunged as in silver.

And by the striped man
directed at the sunny sand
blinked with a click of its black eyelid
12   the camera's ocellus.

That bit of film imprinted
all it could catch,
the stirless child,
16   his radiant mother,

and a toy pail and two beach spades,
and some way off a bank of sand,
and I, the accidental spy,
20   I in the background have been also taken.

Next winter, in an unknown house,
grandmother will be shown an album,
and in that album there will be a snapshot,
24   and in that snapshot I shall be.

мой облик меж людьми чужими,
один мой августовский день,
моя незнаемая ими,
вотще украденная тень.

Бинц, 1927 г.

My likeness among strangers,
one of my August days,
my shade they never noticed,
28   my shade they stole in vain.

Binz, 1927

12
В РАЮ

Моя душа, за смертью дальней
твой образ виден мне вот так:
натуралист провинциальный,
4   в раю потерянный чудак.

Там в роще дремлет ангел дикий,
полупавлинье существо.
Ты любознательно потыкай
8   зеленым зонтиком в него,

соображая, как сначала
о нем напишешь ты статью,
потом... но только нет журнала,
12   и нет читателей в раю.

И ты стоишь, еще не веря
немому горю своему:
об этом синем сонном звере
16   кому расскажешь ты, кому?

Где мир и названные розы,
музей и птичьи чучела? —
и смотришь, смотришь ты сквозь слезы
20   на безымянные крыла.

Берлин, 1927 г.

12
In Paradise

My soul, beyond distant death
your image I see like this:
a provincial naturalist,
an eccentric lost in paradise.

There, in a glade, a wild angel slumbers,
a semi-pavonian creature.
Poke at it curiously
with your green umbrella,

speculating how, first of all,
you will write a paper on it,
then—— But there are no learned journals,
nor any readers in paradise!

And there you stand, not yet believing
your wordless woe.
About that blue somnolent animal
whom will you tell, whom?

Where is the world and the labeled roses,
the museum and the stuffed birds?
And you look and look through your tears
at those unnamable wings.

Berlin, 1927

13
РАССТРЕЛ

Бывают ночи: только лягу,
в Россию поплывет кровать;
и вот ведут меня к оврагу,
4   ведут к оврагу убивать.

Проснусь, и в темноте, со стула,
где спички и часы лежат,
в глаза, как пристальное дуло,
8   глядит горящий циферблат.

Закрыв руками грудь и шею —
вот-вот сейчас пальнет в меня! —
я взгляда отвести не смею
12   от круга тусклого огня.

Оцепенелого сознанья
коснется тиканье часов,
благополучного изгнанья
16   я снова чувствую покров.

Но, сердце, как бы ты хотело,
чтоб это вправду было так:
Россия, звезды, ночь расстрела,
20   и весь в черемухе овраг.

Берлин, 1927

13
The Execution

On certain nights as soon as I lie down
my bed starts drifting into Russia,
and presently I'm led to a ravine,
4   to a ravine led to be killed.

I wake—and in the darkness, from a chair
where watch and matches lie,
into my eyes, like a gun's steadfast muzzle,
8   the glowing dial stares.

With both hands shielding breast and neck—
now any instant it will blast!—
I dare not turn my gaze away
12   from that disk of dull fire.

The watch's ticking comes in contact
with frozen consciousness;
the fortunate protection
16   of my exile I repossess.

But how you would have wished, my heart,
that *thus* it all had really been:
Russia, the stars, the night of execution
20   and full of racemosas the ravine!

Berlin, 1927

Notes

Lines 17–20. Freudians have found here a "death wish," and Marxists, no less grotesquely, "the expiation of feudal guilt." I can assure both groups that the exclamation in this stanza is wholly rhetorical, a trick of style, a deliberately planted surprise, not unlike underpromotion in a chess problem.

"Racemosa" is the name I use for the Russian *cheryomuha*, the "racemose old-world bird cherry," *Padus racemosa* Schneider (see my commentary to *Eugene Onegin*, vol. 3, p. 11).

14
ОТ СЧАСТИЯ ВЛЮБЛЕННОМУ НЕ СПИТСЯ

От счастия влюбленному не спится;
стучат часы; купцу седому снится
в червонном небе вычерченный кран,
4   спускающийся медленно над трюмом;
мерещится изгнанникам угрюмым
в цвет юности окрашенный туман.

В волненьях повседневности прекрасной,
8   где б ни был я, одним я обуян,
одно зовет и мучит ежечасно:

На освещенном острове стола
граненый мрак чернильницы открытой,
12   и белый лист, и лампы свет, забытый
под куполом зеленого стекла.

И поперек листа полупустого
мое перо, как черная стрела,
16   и недописанное слово.

Берлин, 1928 г.

14
For Happiness the Lover Cannot Sleep

For happiness the lover cannot sleep;
the clock ticktacks; the gray-haired merchant fancies
in vermeil skies a silhouetted crane,
into a hold its cargo slowly sinking.
To gloomy exiles there appears miraged
a mist, which youth with its own hue has tinted.

Amidst the agitation and the beauty
of daily life, one image everywhere
haunts me incessantly, torments and claims me:

Upon the bright-lit island of the desk
the somber facets of the open inkstand
and the white sheet of paper, and the lamp's
unswitched-off light beneath its green glass dome.

And left athwart the still half-empty page,
my pen like a black arrow, and the word
I did not finish writing.

Berlin, 1928

15
ЛИЛИТ

Я умер. Яворы и ставни
горячий теребил Эол
вдоль пыльной улицы.
                    Я шел,
4 и фавны шли, и в каждом фавне
я мнил, что Пана узнаю:
«Добро, я, кажется, в раю.»

От солнца заслонясь, сверкая
8 подмышкой рыжею, в дверях
вдруг встала девочка нагая,
с речною лилией в кудрях,
стройна как женщина, и нежно
12 цвели сосцы — и вспомнил я
весну земного бытия,
когда из-за ольхи прибрежной
я близко, близко видеть мог,
16 как дочка мельника меньшая
шла из воды, вся золотая,
с бородкой мокрой между ног.

И вот теперь, в том самом фраке,
20 в котором был вчера убит,
с усмешкой хищною гуляки
я подошел к моей Лилит.
Через плечо зеленым глазом
24 она взглянула — и на мне
одежды вспыхнули и разом
испепелились.

15
Lilith

I died. The sycamores and shutters
along the dusty street were teased
by torrid Aeolus.
               I walked,
4   and fauns walked, and in every faun
god Pan I seemed to recognize:
Good. I must be in Paradise.

Shielding her face and to the sparkling sun
8   showing a russet armpit, in a doorway
there stood a naked little girl.
She had a water lily in her curls
and was as graceful as a woman. Tenderly
12   her nipples bloomed, and I recalled
the springtime of my life on earth,
when through the alders on the river brink
so very closely I could watch
16   the miller's youngest daughter as she stepped
out of the water, and she was all golden,
with a wet fleece between her legs.

And now, still wearing the same dress coat
20   that I had on when killed last night,
with a rake's predatory twinkle,
toward my Lilith I advanced.
She turned upon me a green eye
24   over her shoulder, and my clothes
were set on fire and in a trice
dispersed like ashes.

В глубине

был греческий диван мохнатый,
вино на столике, гранаты,
и в вольной росписи стена.
Двумя холодными перстами
по-детски взяв меня за пламя:
«Сюда,» промолвила она.
Без принужденья, без усилья,
лишь с медленностью озорной,
она раздвинула, как крылья,
свои коленки предо мной.
И обольстителен и весел
был запрокинувшийся лик,
и яростным ударом чресел
я в незабытую проник.
Змея в змее, сосуд в сосуде,
к ней пригнанный, я в ней скользил,
уже восторг в растущем зуде
неописуемый сквозил —
как вдруг она легко рванулась,
отпрянула, и ноги сжав,
вуаль какую-то подняв,
в нее по бедра завернулась,
и полон сил, на полпути
к блаженству, я ни с чем остался
и ринулся и зашатался
от ветра странного. «Впусти!»
я крикнул, с ужасом заметя,
что вновь на улице стою,
и мерзко блеющие дети
глядят на булаву мою.
«Впусти!» — и козлоногий, рыжий

                    In the room behind
            one glimpsed a shaggy Greek divan,
28   on a small table wine, pomegranates,
            and some lewd frescoes covering the wall.
            With two cold fingers childishly
            she took me by my emberhead:
32   "now come along with me," she said.

            Without inducement, without effort,
            Just with the slowness of pert glee,
            like wings she gradually opened
36   her pretty knees in front of me.
            And how enticing, and how merry,
            her upturned face! And with a wild
            lunge of my loins I penetrated
40   into an unforgotten child.
            Snake within snake, vessel in vessel,
            smooth-fitting part, I moved in her,
            through the ascending itch forefeeling
44   unutterable pleasure stir.
            But suddenly she lightly flinched,
            retreated, drew her legs together,
            and grasped a veil and twisted it
48   around herself up to the hips,
            and full of strength, at half the distance
            to rapture, I was left with nothing.
            I hurtled forward. A strange wind
52   caused me to stagger. "Let me in!"
            I shouted, noticing with horror
            that I again stood outside in the dust
            and that obscenely bleating youngsters
56   were staring at my pommeled lust.
            "Let me come in!" And the goat-hoofed,

народ все множился. «Впусти же,
иначе я с ума сойду!»
60   Молчала дверь. И перед всеми
мучительно я пролил семя
и понял вдруг, что я в аду.

Берлин, 1928 г.

copper-curled crowd increased. "Oh, let me in,"
I pleaded, "otherwise I shall go mad!"
60   The door stayed silent, and for all to see
writing with agony I spilled my seed
and knew abruptly that I was in Hell.

Berlin, 1928

Note

Composed more than forty years ago to amuse a friend, "Lilith"
could not be published in any of the sedate *émigré* periodicals of the
time. Its manuscript turned up only recently among my old papers.
Intelligent readers will abstain from examining this impersonal fantasy
for any links with my later fiction.

16
К МУЗЕ

Я помню твой приход: растущий звон,
волнение, неведомое миру.
Луна сквозь ветки тронула балкон,
4   и пала тень, похожая на лиру.

Мне, юному, для неги плеч твоих
казался ямб одеждой слишком грубой.
Но был певуч неправильный мой стих
8   и улыбался рифмой красногубой.

Я счастлив был. Над гаснувшим столом
огонь дрожал, вылущивал огарок;
и снилось мне: страница под стеклом,
12   бессмертная, вся в молниях помарок.

Теперь не то. Для утренней звезды
Не откажусь от утренней дремоты.
Мне не под силу многие труды,
16   особенно — тщеславия заботы.

Я опытен, я скуп и нетерпим.
Натертый стих блистает чище меди.
Мы изредка с тобою говорим
20   через забор, как старые соседи.

Да, зрелость живописна, спору нет:
лист виноградный, груша, пол арбуза
и — мастерства предел — прозрачный свет.
24   Мне холодно. Ведь это осень, муза!

Берлин, 1929

16
The Muse

Your coming I recall: a growing vibrance,
an agitation to the world unknown.
The moon through branches touched the balcony
4   and there a shadow, lyriform, was thrown.

To me, a youth, the iamb seemed a garb
too rude for the soft languor of your shoulders;
but my imperfect line had tunefulness
8   and with the red lips of its rhyme it smiled.

And I was happy. On the dimming desk
a trembling flame hollowed my bit of candle,
and in my dream the page was under glass,
12   immortal, all zigzagged with my corrections.

Not so at present. For the morning star
my morning slumber I will not surrender.
Beyond my strength are multitudes of tasks—
16   especially the worries of ambition.

I am expert, frugal, intolerant.
My polished verse cleaner than copper shines.
We talk occasionally, you and I,
20   across the fence like two old country neighbors.

Yes, ripeness is pictorial, agreed:
leaf of grapevine, pear, watermelon halved,
and—top of artistry—transparent light.
24   I'm feeling cold. Ah, this is autumn, Muse!

Berlin, 1929

17
ТИХИЙ ШУМ

Когда в приморском городке,
средь ночи пасмурной, со скуки
окно откроешь, вдалеке
4   прольются шепчущие звуки.

Прислушайся и различи
шум моря, дышащий на сушу,
оберегающий в ночи
8   ему внимающую душу.

Весь день невнятен шум морской,
но вот проходит день незванный,
позванивая, как пустой
12   стакан на полочке стеклянной.

И вновь в бессонной тишине
открой окно свое пошире,
и с морем ты наедине
16   в огромном и спокойном мире.

Не моря шум — в тиши ночей
иное слышно мне гуденье:
шум тихий родины моей,
20   ее дыханье и биенье.

В нем все оттенки голосов
мне милых, прерванных так скоро,
и пенье пушкинских стихов,
24   и ропот памятного бора.

17
Soft Sound

When in some coastal townlet, on a night
of low clouds and ennui, you open
the window—from afar
4   whispering sounds spill over.

Now listen closely and discern
the sound of seawaves breathing upon land,
protecting in the night
8   the soul that harkens unto them.

Daylong the murmur of the sea is muted,
but the unbidden day now passes
(tinkling as does an empty
12   tumbler on a glass shelf);

and once again amidst the sleepless hush
open your window, wider, wider,
and with the sea you are alone
16   in the enormous and calm world.

Not the sea's sound. . . . In the still night
I hear a different reverberation:
the soft sound of my native land,
20   her respiration and pulsation.

Therein blend all the shades of voices
so dear, so quickly interrupted
and melodies of Pushkin's verse
24   and sighs of a remembered pine wood.

Отдохновенье, счастье в нем,
благословенье над изгнаньем.
Но тихий шум неслышен днем
за суетой и дребезжаньем.

28

Зато в полночной тишине
внимает долго слух неспящий
стране родной, ее шумящей,
ее бессмертной глубине.

32

Ле Булу, 1929 г.

Repose and happiness are there,
a blessing upon exile;
yet the soft sound cannot be heard by day
28   drowned by the scurrying and rattling.

But in the compensating night,
in sleepless silence, one keeps listening
to one's own country, to her murmuring,
32   her deathless deep.

Le Boulou, 1929

18
С Н Е Г

О, этот звук! По-снегу —
скрип, скрип, скрип —
в валенках кто-то идет.

4   Толстый крученый лед
остриями вниз с крыши повис.
Снег скрипуч и блестящ.
(О, этот звук!).

8   Салазки сзади не тащатся —
сами бегут, в пятки бьют.

Сяду и съеду
по крутому, по ровному:
12   валенки врозь,
держусь за веревочку.

Отходя ко сну,
всякий раз думаю:
16   может быть удосужится
меня посетить
тепло одетое, неуклюжее
детство мое.

Берлин, 1930 г.

18
Snow

Oh, that sound! Across snow—
creak, creak, creak:
somebody walking in long boots of felt.

4 Stout, spirally twisted ice,
sharp points inverted, hangs from the eaves.
The snow is crumpy and shiny.
 (Oh, that sound!)

8 My hand sled behind me, far from dragging,
seems to run by itself: it knocks at my heels.

I settle upon it and coast
down the steep, down the smooth:
12 felt boots straddled,
I hold on to the string.

Whenever I'm falling asleep,
I cannot help think:
Maybe you will find a moment
16   to visit me,
my warmly muffled up, clumsy
 childhood.

Berlin, 1930

19
ФОРМУЛА

Сутулится на стуле
беспалое пальто.
Потемки обманули,
почудилось не то.

Сквозняк прошел недавно,
и душу унесло
в раскрывшееся плавно
стеклянное число.

Сквозь отсветы пропущен
сосудов цифровых,
раздут или расплющен
в алембиках кривых,

мой дух преображался:
на тысячу колец,
вращаясь, размножался
и замер наконец

в хрустальнейшем застое,
в отличнейшем Ничто,
а в комнате пустое
сутулится пальто.

Берлин, 1931 г.

19
The Formula

Humped up on the back of a chair,
   a fingerless overcoat.
The darkening day was deceptive:
   fancy has it all wrong.

A current of air has passed recently
   and one's soul has been blown
into a flowingly opening
   cipher of glass.

Filtered through light as reflected
   by the vessels of numbers,
bloated or flattened
   in curved limbs of alembics,

my spirit was being transfigured
   into thousands of rings,
which gyrated and multiplied,
   and at last it all came to a stop,

in most crystal stagnation,
   most excellent Nought;
and in my room just an empty
   overcoat hunches its back.

Berlin, 1931

20
НЕОКОНЧЕННЫЙ ЧЕРНОВИК

Поэт, печалью промышляя,
твердит Прекрасному: прости!
Он говорит, что жизнь земная

4 слова на поднятой в пути
— откуда вырванной? — страницы
(не знаем и швыряем прочь)
или пролет мгновенный птицы

8 чрез светлый зал из ночи в ночь.

Зоил (пройдоха величавый,
корыстью занятый одной)
и литератор площадной

12 (тревожный арендатор славы)
меня страшатся потому,
что зол я, холоден и весел,
что не служу я никому,

16 что жизнь и честь мою я взвесил
на пушкинских весах, и честь
осмеливаюсь предпочесть.

Берлин, 1931 г.

An Unfinished Draft

The poet dealing in Dejection
to Beauty iterates: adieu!
He says that human days are only
4   words on a page picked up by you
upon your way (a page ripped out—
where from? You know not and reject it)
or from the night into the night
8   through a bright hall a brief bird's flight.

Zoilus (a majestic rascal,
whom only lust of gain can stir)
and Publicus, litterateur
12   (a nervous leaseholder of glory),
cower before me in dismay
because I'm wicked, cold, and gay,
because honor and life I weigh
16   on Pushkin's scales and dare prefer
honor. . . .

Berlin, 1931

ВЕЧЕР НА ПУСТЫРЕ

Вдохновенье, розовое небо,
черный дом с одним окном
огненным. О, это небо,
4   выпитое огненным окном!
Загородный сор пустынный,
сорная былинка со слезой,
череп счастья, тонкий, длинный,
8   вроде черепа борзой.
Что со мной? Себя теряю,
растворяюсь в воздухе, в заре;
бормочу и обмираю
12   на вечернем пустыре.
Никогда так плакать не хотелось.
Вот оно, на самом дне.
Донести тебя, чуть запотелое
16   и такое трепетное, в целости
никогда так не хотелось мне.
Выходи, мое прелестное,
зацепись за стебелек,
20   за окно, еще небесное,
иль за первый огонек!
Мир быть может пуст и беспощаден,
я не знаю ничего —
24   но родиться стоит ради
этого дыханья твоего.

Когда-то было легче, проще:
две рифмы — и раскрыл тетрадь.
28   Как смутно в юности заносчивой

21
Evening on a Vacant Lot

In memory of V.D.N.

Inspiration, rosy sky,
black house, with a single window,
fiery. Oh, that sky
4   drunk up by the fiery window!
Trash of solitary outskirts,
weedy little stalk with teardrop,
skull of happiness, long, slender,
8   like the skull of a borzoi.
What's the matter with me? Self-lost,
melting in the air and sunset,
muttering and almost fainting
12   on the waste at eveningtime.
Never did I want so much to cry.
Here it is, deep down in me.
The desire to bring it forth intact,
16   slightly filmed with moisture and so tremulous,
never yet had been so strong in me.
Do come out, my precious being,
cling securely to a stem,
20   to the window, still celestial,
or to the first lighted lamp.
Maybe empty is the world, and brutal;
nothing do I know—except
24   that it's worthwhile being born
for the sake of this your breath.

It once was easier and simpler:
two rhymes—and my notebook I'd open.
28   How hazily I got to know you

мне довелось тебя узнать!
Облокотившись на перила
стиха, плывущего как мост,
32   уже душа вообразила,
что двинулась и заскользила
и доплывет до самых звезд.
Но переписанные начисто,
36   лишась мгновенно волшебства,
бессильно друг за друга прячутся
отяжелевшие слова.

Молодое мое одиночество
40   средь ночных, неподвижных ветвей;
над рекой — изумление ночи,
отраженное полностью в ней;
и сиреневый цвет, бледный баловень
44   этих первых неопытных стоп,
освещенный луной небывалой
в полутрауре парковых троп;
и теперь увеличенный памятью,
48   и прочнее и краше вдвойне,
старый дом, и бессмертное пламя
керосиновой лампы в окне;
и во сне приближение счастия,
52   дальний ветер, воздушный гонец,
все шумней проникающий в чащу,
наклоняющий ветвь наконец;
все, что время как будто и отняло,
56   а глядишь — засквозило опять,
оттого что закрыто неплотно,
и уже невозможно отнять...

Мигая, огненное око
60   глядит сквозь черные персты

in my presumptuous youth!
Leaning my elbows on the railing
of verse that glided like a bridge,
32   already I imagined that my soul
had started moving, started gliding,
and would keep drifting to the very stars.
But when transcribed in a fair copy,
36   deprived of magic instantly,
how helplessly behind each other
the leaden-weighted words would hide!

My young loneliness
40   in the night among motionless boughs!
The amazement of night over the river,
which reflects it in full;
and lilac bloom, the pale darling
44   of my first inexperienced numbers,
with that fabulous moonlight upon it!
And the paths of the park in half-mourning,
and—enlarged at present by memory,
48   twice as solid and beautiful now,
the old house, and the deathless flame
of the kerosene lamp in the window;
and in sleep the nearing of bliss,
52   a far breeze, an aerial envoy
with increasing noise penetrating dense woods,
inclining a branch at last—
all that time had seemed to have taken,
56   but you pause, and again it shines through,
for its lid was not tight—and no longer
can one take it away from you.

Blinking, a fiery eye looks,
60   through the fingerlike black stacks

фабричных труб на сорные цветы
и на жестянку кривобокую.
По пустырю в темнеющей пыли
поджарый пес мелькает шерстью снежной.
Должно быть потерялся. Но вдали
уж слышен свист настойчивый и нежный.
И человек навстречу мне сквозь сумерки
идет, зовет. Я узнаю
походку бодрую твою.
Не изменился ты с тех пор, как умер.

Берлин, 1932

of a factory, at weedy flowers
and a deformed tin can.
Across the vacant lot in darkening dust
64   I glimpse a slender hound with snow-white coat.
Lost, I presume. But in the distance sounds
insistently and tenderly a whistling,
And in the twilight toward me a man
68   comes, calls. I recognize
your energetic stride. You haven't
changed much since you died.

Berlin, 1932

22
БЕЗУМЕЦ

В миру фотограф уличный, теперь же
царь и поэт, парнасский самодержец
(который год сидящий взаперти),
он говорил:

        «Ко славе низойти
я не желал. Она сама примчалась.
Уж я забыл, где муза обучалась,
но путь ее был прям и одинок.
Я не умел друзей готовить впрок,
из лапы льва не извлекал занозы.
Вдруг снег пошел; гляжу, а это розы.

Блаженный жребий. Как мне дорога
унылая улыбочка врага!
Люблю я неудачника тревожить,
сны обо мне мучительные множить
и теневой рассматривать скелет
завистника, прозрачного на свет.

Когда луну я балую балладой,
волнуются деревья за оградой,
вне очереди торопясь попасть
в мои стихи. Доверена мне власть
над всей землей Соседу непослушной,
и счастие так ширится воздушно,
так полнится сияньем голова,
такие совершенные слова
встречают мысль и улетают с нею,
что ничего записывать не смею.

22
The Madman

A street photographer in laic life,
now poet, king, Parnassian autocrat
(since quite a time kept under lock and key),
4   thus did he speak:

               I did not wish to stoop
to Fame: it rushed up of its own accord.
I've now forgotten where my Muse was schooled.
Straight, lonesome was her path. I never knew
8   how to stock friends for use, nor to pull thorns
from lion paws. It suddenly began
to snow; surprising! It was snowing roses.

Enchanting destiny! How much I prize
12   an Enemy's wan little smile! I like
to incommode the Failure, multiply
his painful dreams about me, and examine
the skeleton of Envy, shadowgraphed
16   and showing through, if held up to the light.

When I with balladry blandish the moon
the trees beyond the gate grow agitated
as they endeavor out of turn to get
20   into my verse. I'm privileged to rule
the entire world (which disobeys my Neighbor),
and happiness so airily dilates,
my head is filled with such an incandescence,
24   and words of such impeccable perfection
come to meet Thought and wing away with her
that I dare not write down a single word.

Но иногда — Другим бы стать, другим!
28 О поскорее! Плотником, портным,
а то еще — фотографом бродячим:
как в старой сказке жить, ходить по дачам,
снимать детей пятнистых в гамаке,
32 собаку их и тени на песке.»

Берлин, 1933 г.

Yet sometimes—Oh to be another! Quick!
28   Another! Tailor, carpenter—Or, say,
itinerant photographer: to live
as in an old tale, work the villas, take
pictures of dappled children in a hammock,
32   and of their dog and shadows on the sand.

Berlin, 1933

23
КАК Я ЛЮБЛЮ ТЕБЯ

Такой зеленый, серый, то-есть
весь заштрихованный дождем,
и липовое, столь густое,
4   что я перенести — Уйдем!
Уйдем и этот сад оставим,
и дождь, кипящий на тропах
между тяжелыми цветами,
8   целующими липкий прах.
Уйдем, уйдем, пока не поздно,
скорее, под плащом, домой,
пока еще ты не опознан,
12   безумный мой, безумный мой!

Держусь, молчу. Но с годом каждым,
под гомон птиц и шум ветвей,
разлука та обидней кажется,
16   обида кажется глупей.
И все страшней, что опрометчиво
проговорюсь и перебью
теченье тихой, трудной речи,
20   давно проникшей в жизнь мою.

Над краснощекими рабами
лазурь как лаковая вся,
с накаченными облаками,
24   едва заметными толчками
передвигающимися.
Ужель нельзя там притулиться,
и нет там темного угла,
28   где темнота могла бы слиться
с иероглифами крыла?

23
How I Love You

Kind of green, kind of gray, i.e.,
striated all over with rain,
and the linden fragrance, so heady,

4   that I can hardly—— Let's go!
Let's go and abandon this garden
and the rain that seethes on its paths
between the flowers grown heavy,

8   kissing the sticky loam.
Let's go, let's go before it's too late,
quick, under one cloak, come home,
while you still are unrecognized,

12   my mad one, my mad one!

Self-control, silence. But with each year,
to the murmur of trees and the clamor of birds,
the separation seems more offenseful

16   and the offense more absurd.
And I fear ever more that rashly
I may blab and interrupt
the course of the quiet, difficult speech

20   long since penetrating my life.

Above red-cheeked slaves
the blue sky looks all lacquered,
and pumped-up clouds

24   with scarcely discernible jerks
       move across.
I wonder, is there nowhere a place there,
to lie low—some dark nook

28   where the darkness might merge
with a wing's cryptic markings?

Так бабочка не шевелится,
пластом на плесени ствола.

32 Какой закат! И завтра снова,
и долго-долго быть жаре,
что безошибочно основано
на тишине и мошкаре.

36 В луче вечернем повисая,
она толчется без конца —
как бы игрушка золотая
в руках немого продавца.

40 Как я люблю тебя! Есть в этом
вечернем воздухе порой
лазейки для души, просветы
в тончайшей ткани мировой.

44 Лучи проходят меж стволами.

Как я люблю тебя! Лучи
проходят меж стволами, пламенем
ложатся на стволы. Молчи.

48 Замри под веткою расцветшей,
вдохни, какое разлилось —
зажмурься, уменьшись и в вечное
пройди украдкою насквозь.

Берлин, 1934

(A geometrid thus does not stir
spread flat on a lichened trunk)

32   What a sunset! And once more tomorrow
and for a long time the heat is to last,
a forecast faultlessly based
on the stillness and on the gnats:
36   hanging up in an evening sunbeam,
their swarmlet ceaselessly jiggles,
reminding one of a golden toy
in the hands of a mute peddler.

40   How I love you! In this
evening air, now and then,
the spirit finds loopholes, translucences
in the world's finest texture.
44   The beams pass between tree trunks.

How I love you! The beams
pass between tree trunks; they band
the tree trunks with flame. Do not speak.
48   Stand motionless under the flowering branch,
inhale—what a spreading, what flowing!—
Close your eyes, and diminish, and stealthily
into the eternal pass through.

Berlin, 1934

24

L'INCONNUE DE LA SEINE

Торопя этой жизни развязку,
не любя на земле ничего,
всё гляжу я на белую маску
4   неживого лица твоего.

В без конца замирающих струнах
слышу голос твоей красоты.
В бледных толпах утопленниц юных
8   всех бледней и пленительней ты.

Ты со мною хоть в звуках помешкай,
жребий твой был на счастие скуп,
так ответь же посмертной усмешкой
12   очарованных гипсовых губ.

Неподвижны и выпуклы веки,
густо слиплись ресницы. Ответь,
неужели навеки, навеки?
16   А ведь как ты умела глядеть!

Плечи худенькие, молодые,
черный крест шерстяного платка,
фонари, ветер, тучи ночные,
20   в темных яблоках злая река.

Кто он был, умоляю, поведай,
соблазнитель таинственный твой?
Кудреватый племянник соседа —
24   пестрый галстучек, зуб золотой?

24
L'Inconnue de la Seine

Urging on this life's denouement,
loving nothing upon this earth,
I keep staring at the white mask
4   of your lifeless face.

Strings, vibrating and endlessly dying,
with the voice of your beauty call.
Amidst pale crowds of drowned young maidens
8   you're the palest and sweetest of all.

In music at least linger with me!
Your lot was chary of bliss.
Oh, reply with a posthumous half-smile
12   of your charmed gypsum lips!

Immobile and convex the eyelids.
Thickly matted the lashes. Reply—
can this be for ever, for ever?
16   Ah, the way they could glance, those eyes!

Touchingly frail young shoulders,
the black cross of a woolen shawl,
the streetlights, the wind, the night clouds,
20   the harsh river dappled with dark.

Who was he, I beseech you, tell me,
your mysterious seducer? Was he
some neighbor's curly-locked nephew
24   of the loud tie and gold-capped tooth?

Или звездных небес завсегдатай,
друг бутылки, костей и кия,
вот такой же гуляка проклятый,
прогоревший мечтатель, как я?

И теперь, сотрясаясь всем телом,
он, как я, на кровати сидит
в черном мире, давно опустелом,
и на белую маску глядит.

Берлин, 1934

Or a client of star-dusted heavens,
friend of bottle, billiards, and dice,
the same sort of accursed man of pleasure
28   and bankrupt dreamer as I?

And right now, his whole body heaving,
he, like me, on the edge of his bed,
in a black world long empty, sits staring
32   at a white mask?

Berlin, 1934

25
НА ЗАКАТЕ

На закате, у той же скамьи,
как во дни молодые мои,

на закате, ты знаешь каком,
с яркой тучей и майским жуком,

у скамьи, с полусгнившей доской,
высоко над румяной рекой,

как тогда, в те далекие дни,
улыбнись и лицо отверни,

если душам умерших давно
иногда возвращаться дано.

Берлин, 1935

25
At Sunset

At sunset, by the same bench,
as in the days of my youth,

At sunset, you know the kind,
with a bright-colored cloud and a chafer,

At the bench with the half-rotten board,
high above the incarnadine river,

As then, in those distant days,
smile and avert your face,

If to souls of those long dead
it is given sometimes to return.

Berlin, 1935

26
МЫ С ТОБОЮ ТАК ВЕРИЛИ

Мы с тобою так верили в связь бытия,
но теперь оглянулся я — и удивительно,
до чего ты мне кажешься, юность моя,
4   по цветам не моей, по чертам недействительной!

Если вдуматься, это — как дымка волны
между мной и тобой, между мелью и тонущим;
или вижу столбы и тебя со спины,
8   как ты прямо в закат на своем полугоночном.

Ты давно уж не я, ты набросок, герой
всякой первой главы — а как долго нам верилось
в непрерывность пути от ложбины сырой
12   до нагорного вереска.

Париж, 1938

26
We So Firmly Believed

We so firmly believed in the linkage of life,
but now I've looked back—and it is astonishing
to what a degree you, my youth,
4   seem in tints not mine, in traits not real.

If one probes it, it's rather like a wave's haze
between me and you, between shallow and sinking,
or else I see telegraph poles and you from the back
8   as right into the sunset you ride your half-racer.

You've long ceased to be I. You're an outline—the
       hero
of any first chapter; yet how long we believed
that there was no break in the way from the damp
       dell
12   to the alpine heath.

Paris, 1938

ЧТО ЗА-НОЧЬ

Что за-ночь с памятью случилось?
Снег выпал, что-ли? Тишина.
Душа забвенью зря училась:
4   во сне задача решена.

Решенье чистое, простое,
(о чем я думал столько лет?).
Пожалуй, и вставать не стоит:
8   ни тела, ни постели нет.

Ментона, 1938

What Happened Overnight

What happened overnight to memory?
It must have snowed: such stillness! Of no use
Was to my soul the study of Oblivion:
4   that problem has been solved in sleep.

A simple, elegant solution.
(Now what have I been bothering about
so many years?) One does not see much need
8   in getting up: there's neither bed, nor body.

Mentone, 1938

28
ПОЭТЫ

Из комнаты в сени свеча переходит
и гаснет. Плывет отпечаток в глазах,
пока очертаний своих не находит
беззвездная ночь в темно-синих ветвях.

4

Пора, мы уходим — еще молодые,
со списком еще неприснившихся снов,
с последним, чуть зримым сияньем России
на фосфорных рифмах последних стихов.

8

А мы ведь, поди, вдохновение знали,
нам жить бы, казалось, и книгам расти,
но музы безродные нас доканали,
и ныне пора нам из мира уйти.

12

И не потому, что боимся обидеть
своею свободою добрых людей.
Нам просто пора, да и лучше не видеть
всего, что сокрыто от прочих очей:

16

не видеть всей муки и прелести мира,
окна в отдаленьи поймавшего луч,
лунатиков смирных в солдатских мундирах,
высокого неба, внимательных туч;

20

красы, укоризны; детей малолетних,
играющих в прятки вокруг и внутри
уборной, кружащейся в сумерках летних;
красы, укоризны вечерней зари;

24

28
The Poets

From room to hallway a candle passes
and is extinguished. Its imprint swims in one's eyes,
until, among the blue-black branches,
4   a starless night its contours finds.

It is time, we are going away: still youthful,
with a list of dreams not yet dreamt,
with the last, hardly visible radiance of Russia
8   on the phosphorent rhymes of our last verse.

And yet we did know—didn't we?—inspiration,
we would live, it seemed, and our books would grow,
but the kithless muses at last have destroyed us,
12   and it is time now for us to go.

And this not because we're afraid of offending
with our freedom good people; simply, it's time
for us to depart—and besides we prefer not
16   to see what lies hidden from other eyes;

not to see all this world's enchantment and torment,
the casement that catches a sunbeam afar,
humble somnambulists in soldier's uniform,
20   the lofty sky, the attentive clouds;

the beauty, the look of reproach; the young children
who play hide-and-seek inside and around
the latrine that revolves in the summer twilight;
24   the sunset's beauty, its look of reproach;

всего, что томит, обвивается, ранит;
рыданья рекламы на том берегу,
текучих ее изумрудов в тумане,
28 всего, что сказать я уже не могу.

Сейчас переходим с порога мирского
в ту область... как хочешь ее назови:
пустыня ли, смерть, отрешенье от слова,
32 иль, может быть, проще; молчанье любви.

Молчанье далекой дороги тележной,
где в пене цветов колея не видна,
молчанье отчизны — любви безнадежной —
36 молчанье зарницы, молчанье зерна.

Париж, 1939

all that weighs upon one, entwines one, wounds one;
an electric sign's tears on the opposite bank;
through the mist the stream of its emeralds running;
28   all the things that already I cannot express.

In a moment we'll pass across the world's threshold
into a region—name it as you please:
wilderness, death, disavowal of language,
32   or maybe simpler: the silence of love;

the silence of a distant cartway, its furrow,
beneath the foam of flowers concealed;
my silent country (the love that is hopeless);
36   the silent sheet lightning, the silent seed.

Paris, 1939

Notes

The poem was published in a magazine under the pseudonym of
"Vasiliy Shishkov" in order to catch a distinguished critic (G.
Adamovich, of the *Poslednie novosti*) who automatically objected to
everything I wrote. The trick worked: in his weekly review he wel-
comed the appearance of a mysterious new poet with such eloquent
enthusiasm that I could not resist keeping up the joke by describing
my meetings with the fictitious Shishkov in a story which contained,
among other plums, a criticism of the poem and of Adamovich's
praise.

26–27. The streaming emeralds of an aspirin advertisement on the other
side of the Seine.

К РОССИИ

29

Отвяжись — я тебя умоляю!
Вечер страшен, гул жизни затих.
Я беспомощен. Я умираю
от слепых наплываний твоих.

Тот, кто вольно отчизну покинул,
волен выть на вершинах о ней,
но теперь я спустился в долину,
и теперь приближаться не смей.

Навсегда я готов затаиться
и без имени жить. Я готов,
чтоб с тобой и во снах не сходиться,
отказаться от всяческих снов;

обескровить себя, искалечить,
не касаться любимейших книг,
променять на любое наречье
всё, что есть у меня, — мой язык.

Но зато, о Россия, сквозь слезы,
сквозь траву двух несмежных могил,
сквозь дрожащие пятна березы,
сквозь всё то, чем я смолоду жил,

дорогими слепыми глазами
не смотри на меня, пожалей,
не ищи в этой угольной яме,
не нащупывай жизни моей!

29
To Russia

Will you leave me alone? I implore you!
Dusk is ghastly. Life's noises subside.
I am helpless. And I am dying
4   Of the blind touch of your whelming tide.

He who freely abandons his country
on the heights to bewail it is free.
But now I am down in the valley
8   and now do not come close to me.

I'm prepared to lie hidden forever
and to live without name. I'm prepared,
lest we only in dreams come together,
12   all conceivable dreams to forswear;

to be drained of my blood, to be crippled,
to have done with the books I most love,
for the first available idiom
16   to exchange all I have: my own tongue.

But for that, through the tears, oh, Russia,
through the grass of two far-parted tombs,
through the birchtree's tremulous macules,
20   through all that sustained me since youth,

with your blind eyes, your dear eyes, cease looking
at me, oh, pity my soul,
do not rummage around in the coalpit,
24   do not grope for my life in this hole

Ибо годы прошли и столетья,
и за горе, за муку, за стыд
— поздно, поздно! — никто не ответит,
и душа никому не простит.

28

Париж, 1939

because years have gone by and centuries,
and for sufferings, sorrow, and shame,
too late—there is no one to pardon

28   and no one to carry the blame.

Paris, 1939

Note

The original, a streamlined, rapid mechanism, consists of regular three-
foot anapests of the "panting" type, with alternating feminine-mascu-
line rhymes. It was impossible to combine lilt and literality, except in
some passages (only the third stanza gives a close imitation of the
poem's form); and since the impetus of the original redeems its verbal
vagueness, my faithful but bumpy version is not the success that a
prosy cab might have been.

30
О К О

К одному исполинскому оку
без лица, без чела и без век,
без телесного марева сбоку,
наконец-то сведен человек.

И на землю без ужаса глянув
(совершенно не схожую с той,
что, вся пегая от океанов,
улыбалась одною щекой),

он не горы там видит, не волны,
не какой-нибудь яркий залив,
и не кинематограф безмолвный
облаков, виноградников, нив;

и конечно не угол столовой
и свинцовые лица родных —
ничего он не видит такого
в тишине обращений своих.

Дело в том, что исчезла граница
между вечностью и веществом —
и на что неземная зеница,
если вензеля нет ни на чем?

Париж, 1939 г.

30
Oculus

To a single colossal oculus,
without lids, without face, without brow,
without halo of marginal flesh,
4   man is finally limited now.

And without any fear having glanced
at the earth (quite unlike the old freak
that was dappled all over with seas
8   and smiled with the sun on one cheek),

not mountains he sees and not waves,
not some gulf that brilliantly shines,
and not the silent old cinema
12   of clouds, and grainfields, and vines,

and of course not a part of the parlor
with his kin's leaden faces—oh, no,
in the stillness of his revolutions
16   nothing in that respect will he know.

Gone, in fact, is the break between matter
and eternity; and who can care
for a world of omnipotent vision,
20   if nothing is monogrammed there?

Paris, 1939

31
С Л А В А

И вот как на колесиках вкатывается ко мне некто
восковой, поджарый, с копотью в красных
      ноздрях,
и сижу, и решить не могу: человек это,
4   или просто так — разговорчивый прах.
Как проситель из наглых, гроза общежитий,
как зловещий друг детства, как старший шпион
(шепелявым таким шопотком: а скажите,
8   что вы делали там-то?), как сон,
как палач, как шпион, как друг детства зловещий,
как в балканской новелле влиянье — как их,
символистов — но хуже. Есть вещи, вещи,
12   которые... даже... (Акакий Акакиевич
любил, если помните, «плевелы речи»,
и он, как Наречье, мой гость восковой),
и сердце просится, и сердце мечется,
16   и я не могу. — А его разговор
так и катится острою осыпью под гору,
и картавое, кроткое слушать должно
и заслушиваться господина бодрого,
20   оттого, что без слов и без славы оно.
Как пародия совести в драме бездарной,
как палач и озноб и последний рассвет —

31
Fame

1

And now there rolls in, as on casters, a character,
waxlike, lean-loined, with red nostrils soot-stuffed,
and I sit and cannot decide: is it human
4   or nothing special—just garrulous dust?

Like a blustering beggar, the pest of the poorhouse,
like an evil old schoolmate, like the head spy
(in that thick slurred murmur: "Say, what were you
            doing
8   in such and such place?"), like a dream,

like a spy, like a hangman, like an evil old school-
            mate,
like the Influence on the Balkan Novella of—er—
the Symbolist School, only worse. There are matters,
            matters,
12   which, so to speak, even . . . (Akakiy Akakievich

had a weakness, if you remember, for "weed words,"
and he's like an Adverb, my waxy guest),
and my heart keeps pressing, and my heart keeps
            tossing,
16   and I can't any more—while his speech

fairly tumbles on downhill, like sharp loose gravel,
and the burry-R'd meek heart must harken to him,
aye, harken entranced to the buoyant gentleman
20   because it has got no words and no fame.

Like a mockery of conscience in a cheap drama,
like a hangman, and shiverings, and the last dawn—

— о, волна, поднимись, тишина благодарна
24 и за эту трехсложную музыку. — Нет,
не могу языку заказать эти звуки,
ибо гость говорит — и так веско,
господа, и так весело, и на гадюке
28 то панама, то шлем, то фуражка, то феска:
иллюстрации разных существенных доводов,
головные уборы, как мысли во-вне;
или, может быть — Было бы здорово,
32 если б этим шутник указывал мне,
что я страны менял, как фальшивые деньги,
торопясь и боясь оглянуться назад,
как раздваивающееся привиденье,
36 как свеча меж зеркал уплывая в закат.
Далеко до лугов, где ребенком я плакал,
упустив аполлона, и дальше еще
до еловой аллеи с полосками мрака,
40 меж которыми полдень сквозил горячо.
Но воздушным мостом мое слово изогнуто
через мир, и чредой спицевидных теней
без конца по нему прохожу я инкогнито
44 в полыхающий сумрак отчизны моей.
Я божком себя вижу, волшебником с птичьей
головой, в изумрудных перчатках, в чулках
из лазурных чешуй. Прохожу. Перечтите
48 и остановитесь на этих строках.

Oh, wave, swell up higher! The stillness is grateful
for the least bit of ternary music—— No, gone!

I can't make my tongue conform to those accents,
for my visitor speaks—and so weightily, folks,
and so cheerfully, and the creep wears in turn
a panama hat, a cap, a helmet, a fez:

illustrations of various substantial arguments,
headgear in the sense of externalized thought?
Or maybe—oh, that would be really something
if thereby the clown indicated to me

that I kept changing countries like counterfeit money,
hurrying on and afraid to look back,
like a phantom dividing in two, like a candle
between mirrors sailing into the low sun.

It is far to the meadows where I sobbed in my child-
hood
heaving missed an Apollo, and farther yet
to the alley of firs where the midday sunlight
glowed with fissures of fire between bands of jet.

But my word, curved to form an aerial viaduct,
spans the world, and across in a strobe-effect spin
of spokes I keep endlessly passing incognito
into the flame-licked night of my native land.

To myself I appear as an idol, a wizard
bird-headed, emerald gloved, dressed in tights
made of bright-blue scales. I pass by. Reread it
and pause for a moment to ponder these lines.

24
28
32
36
40
44
48

Обращение к несуществующим: Кстати,
он не мост, этот шорох, а цепь облаков,
и лишенные самой простой благодати
(дохожденья до глаз, до локтей, до висков),
«твои бедные книги», сказал он развязно,
«безнадежно растают в изгнаньи. Увы,
эти триста листов беллетристики праздной
разлетятся — но у настоящей листвы
есть куда упадать, есть земля, есть Россия,
есть тропа вся в лиловой кленовой крови,
есть порог, где слоятся тузы золотые,
есть канавы — а бедные книги твои
без земли, без тропы, без канав, без порога,
опадут в пустоте, где ты вырастил ветвь,
как базарный факир, то-есть не без подлога,
и не долго ей в дымчатом воздухе цвесть.
Кто в осеннюю ночь, кто, скажи-ка на милость,
в захолустии русском, при лампе, в пальто,
среди гильз папиросных, каких-то опилок,
и других озаренных неясностей, кто
на столе развернет образец твоей прозы,
зачитается ею под шум дождевой,
набегающий шум заоконной березы,
поднимающей книгу на уровень свой?

52
56
60
64
68
72

Addressed to non-beings. Apropos, that shuffle
is no viaduct, but a procession of clouds,
and deprived of the simplest of possible blessings
(reaching up to the elbows, the temples, the eyes),

52

"Your poor books," he breezily said, "will finish
by hopelessly fading in exile. Alas,
those two thousand leaves of frivolous fiction
will be scattered; but genuine foliage has

56

a place where to fall: there's the soil, there's Russia,
there's a path drenched by maples in violet blood,
there's a threshold where lie overlapping gold aces,
there are ditches; but your unfortunate books

60

without soil, without path, without ditch, without
     threshold,
will be shed in a void where you brought forth a
     branch,
as bazaar fakirs do (that is, not without faking),
and not long will it bloom in the smoke-colored air.

64

Who, some autumn night, *who*, tell us, please, in the
     backwoods
of Russia, by lamplight, in his overcoat,
amidst cigarette gills, miscellaneous sawdust,
and other illumed indiscernibles—who

68

on the table a sample of *your* prose will open,
absorbed, will read *you* to the noise of the rain,
to the noise of the birch tree that rushes up window-
     ward
and to its own level raises the book?

72

Нет, никто никогда на просторе великом
ни одной не помянет страницы твоей:
ныне дикий пребудет в неведеньи диком,
друг степей для тебя не забудет степей.

В длинном стихотворении «Слава» — писателя,
так сказать, занимает проблема, гнетет
мысль о контакте с сознаньем читателя.

К сожаленью, и это навек пропадет.
Повторяй же за мной, дабы в сладостной язве
до конца, до небес доскрестись: никогда,
никогда не мелькнет мое имя — иль разве

(как в трагических тучах мелькает звезда)
в специальном труде, в примечаньи к названью
эмигрантского кладбища, и наравне
с именами собратьев по правописанью,

обстоятельством места навязанных мне.
Повторил? А случалось еще, ты пописывал
не без блеска на вовсе чужом языке,
и припомни особенный привкус анисовый

тех потуг, те метанья в словесной тоске.
И виденье: на родине. Мастер. Надменность.
Непреклонность. Но тронуть не смеют. Порой
перевод иль отрывок. Поклонники. Ценность

европейская. Дача в Алуште. Герой».

No, never will anyone in the great spaces
make mention of even one page of your work;
the now savage will dwell in his savage ignorance,
friends of steppes won't forget their steppes for your
76   sake."

In a long piece of poetry, "Fame," the author
is concerned, so to speak, with the problem, is irked
by the thought of contacting the reader's aware-
   ness. . . .
80 "This too, I'm afraid, will vanish for good.

So repeat after me (as one rakes a delicious
sore to get to the end, to its heaven): Not once,
not once will my name come up briefly, save maybe
84 —as a star briefly passing among tragic clouds—

In a specialist's work, in a note to the title
of some *émigré* churchyard and on a par
with the names of my co-orthographical brethren
88 which a matter of locus had forced upon me.

Repeated? And furthermore, not without brio,
you happened to write in some quite foreign tongue.
You recall the particular anise-oil flavor
92 of those strainings, those flingings in verbal distress?

And a vision : you are in your country. Great writer.
Proud. Unyielding. But no one dares touch you. At
   times,
A translation or fragment. Admirers. All Europe
96 Esteems you. A villa near Yalta. A hero."

И тогда я смеюсь, и внезапно с пера
        мой любимый слетает анапест,
образуя ракеты в ночи — так быстра
100   золотая становится запись.

И я счастлив. Я счастлив, что совесть моя,
        сонных мыслей и умыслов сводня,
не затронула самого тайного. Я
104   ·   удивительно счастлив сегодня.

Эта тайна та-та, та-та-та-та, та-та,
        а точнее сказать я не вправе.

Оттого так смешна мне пустая мечта
108   о читателе, теле и славе.

Я без тела разросся, без отзвука жив,
        и со мной моя тайна всечасно.

Что мне тление книг, если даже разрыв
112   между мной и отчизною — частность?

Признаюсь, хорошо зашифрована ночь,
        но под звезды я буквы подставил
и в себе прочитал чем себя превозмочь,
116   а точнее сказать, я не вправе.

Не доверясь соблазнам дороги большой
        или снам, освященным веками,
остаюсь я безбожником с вольной душой
120   в этом мире, кишащем богами.

Then I laugh, and at once from my pen nib a flight
 of my favorite anapaests rises,
in the night making rocket streaks with the increase
100 in the speed of the golden inscribing.

And I'm happy. I'm happy that Conscience, the pimp
 of my sleepy reflections and projects,
did not get at the critical secret. Today
104 I am really remarkably happy.

That main secret tra-tá-ta tra-tá-ta tra-tá—
 and I must not be overexplicit;
this is why I find laughable the empty dream
108 about readers, and body, and glory.

Without body I've spread, without echo I thrive,
 and with me all along is my secret.
A book's death can't affect me since even the break
112 between me and my land is a trifle.

I admit that the night has been ciphered right well
 but in place of the stars I put letters,
and I've read in myself how the self to transcend—
116 and I must not be overexplicit.

Trusting not the enticements of the thoroughfare
 or such dreams as the ages have hallowed,
I prefer to stay godless, with fetterless soul
120 in a world that is swarming with godheads.

Но однажды, пласты разуменья дробя,
углубляясь в свое ключевое,
я увидел, как в зеркале, мир, и себя,
и другое, другое, другое.

Уэльслей (Масс.), 1942

But one day while disrupting the strata of sense
and descending deep down to my wellspring
I saw mirrored, besides my own self and the world,
something else, something else, something else.

124

Wellesley, Massachusetts, 1942

Notes

Line 12/ *Akakiy Akakievich.* The hero of Gogol's *Shinel'* (The Carrick) whose speech was interspersed with more or less meaningless accessory words.

Line 42/ *strobe-effect spin.* The term renders exactly what I tried to express by the looser phrase in my text "sequence of spokelike shadows." The strobe effect causes wheels to look as if they revolved backward, and the crossing over to America (line 36) becomes an optical illusion of a return to Russia.

Lines 47–48. The injunction is addressed to those—probably nonexisting—readers who might care to decipher an allusion in lines 45–47 to the *sirin,* a fabulous fowl of Slavic mythology, and "Sirin," the author's penname in his 1920–1940 period.

Line 67/ *gill.* The carton mouthpiece of a Russian cigarette. An unswept floor in a cold room strewn all over with the tubes of discarded cigarette butts used to be a typical platform for the meditations of a hard-up Russian enthusiast in the idealistic past.

Lines 75–76. The references here are to the third stanza of Pushkin's "*Exegi monumentum*" (1836):

Tidings of me will cross the whole great Rus,
and name me will each tribe existing there:
proud scion of Slavs, and Finn, and the now savage
Tungus, and—friend of steppes—the Kalmuck

Line 87/ *co-orthographical brethren.* A new orthography was introduced in 1917, but *émigré* publications stuck to the old one.

Line 91/ *anise-oil.* An allusion to the false fox scent, a drag fooling hounds into following it in lieu of the game.

32
ПАРИЖСКАЯ ПОЭМА

«Отведите, но только не бросьте!
Это — люди; им жалко Москвы.
Позаботьтесь об этом прохвосте:

4   он когда-то был ангел, как вы.
И подайте крыло Никанору,
Аврааму, Владимиру, Льву —
смерду, князю, предателю, вору:

8   Ils furent des anges comme vous.
Всю ораву — ужасные выи
стариков у чужого огня —
господа, господа голубые,

12   пожалейте вы ради меня!

От кочующих, праздно плутающих
уползаю — и вот привстаю,
и уже я лечу, и на тающих

16   рифмы нет в моем новом раю.
Потому-то я вправе по чину
к вам, бряцая, в палаты войти.
Хорошо. Понимаю причину —

20   но их надо, их надо спасти!
Хоть бы вы призадумались, хоть бы
согласились взглянуть — А пока
остаюсь с привидением (подпись

24   неразборчива: ночь, облака)».

The Paris Poem

1

"Lead them off, only do not discard them!
They are human. Their Moscow they rue.
Give some thought to the needs of that scoundrel:
He was once an angel like you.

And extend a wing to Nicander,
Abram, Vladimir, and Leo, too;
to the slave, prince, traitor, bandit:
ils furent des anges comme vous.

The whole crew—at an alien fireside
(those ghastly necks of old men):
masters, my azure masters,
for my sake have pity on them!

2

From those wandering, those idly straying,
I now crawl away, and now rise,
and I'm flying at last—and 'dissolving'
has no rhyme in my new paradise.

That is how by rank I'm entitled
with loud clangor to enter your hall.
Very well. I'm aware of the reason—
but they *must* be rescued all!

You at least might reflect, you at least might
condescend to glance briefly—Meanwhile
I remain your specterful (signature
illegible. Night. Cloudy sky)."

Так он думал без воли, без веса,
сам в себя, как наследник, летя.
Ночь дышала: вздувалась завеса,
облакам облаками платя.
Стул. На стуле он сам. На постели
снова — он. В бездне зеркала — он.
Он — в углу, он — в полу, он — у цели,
он в себе, он в себе, он спасен.

А теперь мы начнем. Жил в Париже,
в пятом доме по рю Пьер Лоти,
некто Вульф, худощавый и рыжий
инженер лет пятидесяти.
А под ним — мой герой: тот писатель,
о котором писал я не раз,
мой приятель, мой работодатель.

Посмотрев на часы — и сквозь час
дно и камушки мельком увидя,
он оделся и вышел. У нас
это дно называлось: Овидий
откормлен (от «Carmina»). Муть
и комки в голове после черной
стихотворной работы. Чуть-чуть
моросит, и над улицей черной
без звездинки муругая муть.
Но поэмы не будет: нам некуда
с ним итти. По ночам он гулял.
Не любил он ходить к человеку,
а хорошего зверя не знал.

3

Thus he thought without willing it, weightless,
while into himself, like an heir, he flew.
The night breathed. The window drape billowed
28   with clouds paying clouds their due.

Chair. He on the chair. Bed. Upon it
he again. Mirror. He in its gulf.
He in the corner. He in the floor. At the finish.
32   In himself, in himself. Safe!

4

And now we begin. There dwelt in Paris,
number five on rue Pierre Loti,
one Vulf, a red-haired, lanky
36   civil engineer aged fifty-three.

And under him lived my hero, the author
whom I've written about more than once.
My pal, my employer.

5

40   Having looked at his watch and glimpsed
through the hour its pebble-strewn bottom,
he dressed and went out. He and I
dubbed that bottom: "Ovidius
44   crammed with *carmina*." Mist
and clods in the head after hideous
verse-making labor. A slight
drizzle outside, and above the black street
48   not the faintest star in the marron mist.
But there will be no poem: We've nowhere
to go. At night he would ramble.
He did not like visiting people
52   and did not know any nice animal.

С этим камнем ночным породниться,
пить извозчичье это вино...
Трясогузками ходят блудницы,
и на русском Парнасе темно.
Вымирают косматые мамонты,
чуть жива красноглазая мышь.
Бродят отзвуки лиры безграмотной:
с кандачка переход на Буль-Миш.
С полурусского, полузабытого
переход на подобье арго.
Бродит боль позвонка перебитого
в черных дебрях Бульвар Араго.
Ведь последняя капля России
уже высохла! Будет, пойдем!
Но еще подписаться мы силимся
кривоклювым почтамтским пером.

Чуден ночью Париж сухопарый...
Чу! Под сводами черных аркад,
где стена как скала, писсуары
за щитами своими журчат.
Есть судьба и альпийское нечто
в этом плеске пустынном. Вот-вот
захлебнется меж четом и нечетом,
между мной и не мной, счетовод.
А мосты — Это счастье навеки,
счастье черной воды. Посмотри:

6

To be one with this stone which is one with
      night,
to drink this red wine, which the cabby drinks.
And the whores, they walk as the wagtails walk,
56   And the Russian Parnassus in darkness sinks.

Dying out are the shaggy mammoths,
Barely alive is the red-eyed mouse.
Echoes of an illiterate lyre here wander,
60   from the slipshod to Boul'Mich you pass.

From a tongue half-Russin and half-forgotten
here you pass to a form of *argot*.
The pain of a severed vertebra wanders
64   in the black depths of Boulevard Arago.

Hasn't the very last inkdrop of Russia
already dried up? Let's be going then.
Yet we still attempt to scrawl our signature
68   with a crooked-beaked post-office pen.

7

Wondrous at night is gaunt Paris.
Hark! Under the vaults of black arcades,
where the walls are rocklike, the urinals
72   gurgle behind their shields.

There is Fate and an alpine something
in that desolate splash. Any moment now,
between even and odd, between me and non-me,
76   that keeper of records will choke and drown.

And the bridges! That's bliss everlasting,
the bliss of black water. Look, what a sight:

как стекло несравненной аптеки
80   — и оранжевые фонари.
А вверху — Там неважные вещи.
Без конца. Без конца. Только муть.
Мертвый в омуте месяц мерещится.
84   Неужели я тоже? Забудь.
Смерть еще далека (послезавтра я
все продумаю), но иногда
сердцу хочется «автора, автора!».
88   В зале автора нет, господа.
И покуда глядел он на месяц,
синеватый, как кровоподтек,
раздался, где-то в дальнем предместье,
92   паровозный щемящий свисток.
Лист бумаги, громадный и чистый,
стал вытаскивать он из себя:
лист был больше него и неистовствовал,
96   завиваясь в трубу и скрипя.
И борьба показалась запутанной,
безысходной: я, черная мгла,
я, огни, и вот эта минута —
100   и вот эта минута прошла.
Но как знать — может быть бесконечно
драгоценна она, и потом
пожалею, что бесчеловечно
104   обошелся я с этим листом.
Что-нибудь мне быть может напели
эти камни и дальний свисток.

the vitrine of an incomparable pharmacy
80   and the globes of lamps full of orange light.

Overhead—matters there are less pretty
Without end. Without end. Just a mist.
A dead moon phantasmed in its millpool.
84   Can it be that I too—? Dismissed.

Death is distant yet (after tomorrow
I'll think everything through); but now and then
one's heart starts clamoring: Author! Author!
88   He is not in the house, gentlemen.

And while I looked at the crescent
as blue as a bruise, there came
from a distant suburb, the whistle
92   —heartrending sound!—of a train.

A huge clean sheet of paper I started
to extract from myself. The sheet
was bigger than me and frenetically
96   it rolled up in a funnel and creaked.

And the struggle began to seem muddled,
unresolvable: I, the black sky,
I, the lights, and the present minute—
100   and the present minute went by.

But who knows—perhaps, it was priceless
and perhaps I'd regret some day
having treated that sheet of paper
104   in such an inhuman way.

Perhaps something to me they incanted—
those stones and that whistle afar?

И пошарив по темной панели,
108   он нашел свой измятый листок.

В этой жизни, богатой узорами
(неповторной, поскольку она
по-другому, с другими актерами,
112   будет в новом театре дана),
я почел бы за лучшее счастье
так сложить ее дивный ковер,
чтоб пришелся узор настоящего
116   на былое — на прежний узор;
чтоб опять очутиться мне — о, не
в общем месте хотений таких,
не на карте России, не в лоне
120   ностальгических неразберих —
но с далеким найдя соответствие,
очутиться в начале пути,
наклониться — и в собственном детстве
124   кончик спутанной нити найти.
И распутать себя осторожно,
как подарок, как чудо, и стать
серединою многодорожного
128   громогласного мира опять.
И по яркому гомону птичьему,
по ликующим липам в окне,
по их зелени преувеличенной,
132   и по солнцу на мне и во мне,

And on the sidewalk groping, my crumpled
108   scrap of paper I found in the dark.

                                    8
In this life, rich in patterns (a life
unrepeatable, since with a different
cast, in a different manner,
112   in a new theater it will be given),

no better joy would I choose than to fold
its magnificent carpet in such a fashion
as to make the design of today coincide
116   with the past, with a former pattern,

in order to visit again—oh, not
commonplaces of those inclinations,
not the map of Russia, and not a lot
120   of nostalgic equivocations—

but, by finding congruences with the remote,
to revisit my fountainhead,
to bend and discover in my own childhood
124   the end of the tangled-up thread.

And carefully then to unravel myself
as a gift, as a marvel unfurled,
and become once again the middle point
128   of the many-pathed, loud-throated world.

And by the bright din of the birds
by the jubilant window-framed lindens
by their extravagant greenery,
132   by the sunlight upon me and in me,

и по белым гигантам в лазури,
что стремятся ко мне напрямик,
по сверканью, по мощи — прищуриться
и узнать свой сегодняшний миг.

Кембридж (Масс.), 1943

by the white colossi that rush through the blue
straight at me—as I narrow my eyes—
by all that sparkle and all that power
my present moment to recognize.

136

Cambridge, Massachusetts, 1943

Notes

13/*Ot kochúyushchih, prázdno plutáyushchih.*
The original imitates much more closely Nekrasov's line calling the poet away "from those jubilant, those idly babbling" (*ot likuyúshchih, prázdno boltáyushchih*) to the camp (*stan*) of those revolutionaries "who perish in the name of the great deed of love." Nikolay Alekseevich Nekrasov, 1821–77, a famous poet who successfully transcended, in a few great poems, the journalist in him, who wrote topical jingles.

23/ *ostayus's privideniem.* Lexically: "I remain with specter," a play on the closing cliché of *ostayus s uvazheniem,* "I remain with respect." Every now and then fidelity receives a miraculous reward.

25–26/ *Thus he thought* . . . An allusion to Pushkin's *Eugene Onegin,* first four lines of second stanza:

> Thus a young scapegrace thought,
> with posters flying in dust,
> by the most lofty will of Zeus
> the heir of all his relatives.

64/*Boulevard Arago.* Until quite recently it was there that public decapitations took place in Paris, with local grocers getting the closest view of a reasonably sensational but generally rather messy show.

69/*Chuden noch'yu Parizh.* An imitation of a hyperbolic passage in Gogol's *A Terrible Vengeance* (a wretchedly corny tale) which begins: *Chuden Dnepr pri tihoy pogode,* "wondrous is the Dnepr in windless weather."

33
КАКИМ БЫ ПОЛОТНОМ

Каким бы полотном батальным ни являлась
советская сусальнейшая Русь,
какой бы жалостью душа ни наполнялась,
   не поклонюсь, не примирюсь

4

со всею мерзостью, жестокостью и скукой
немого рабства — нет, о, нет,
еще я духом жив, еще не сыт разлукой,
   увольте, я еще поэт.

8

Кембридж, Массачусеттс, 1944 г.

33
No Matter How

No matter how the Soviet tinsel glitters
upon the canvas of a battle piece;
no matter how the soul dissolves in pity,
I will not bend, I will not cease

loathing the filth, brutality, and boredom
of silent servitude. No, no, I shout,
my spirit is still quick, still exile-hungry,
I'm still a poet, count me out!

Cambridge, Massachusetts, 1944

О ПРАВИТЕЛЯХ

Вы будете (как иногда
говорится)
смеяться, вы будете (как ясновидцы
4   говорят) хохотать, господа —
но, честное слово,
у меня есть приятель,
которого
8   привела бы в волнение мысль поздороваться
с главою правительства или другого какого
предприятия.
С каких это пор, желал бы я знать,
12   подложечкой
мы стали испытывать вроде
нежного бульканья, глядя в бинокль
на плотного с ежиком в ложе?
16   С каких это пор
понятие власти стало равно
ключевому понятию родины?
Какие-то римляне и мясники,
20   Карл Красивый и Карл Безобразный,
совершенно гнилые князьки,
толстогрудые немки и разные
людоеды, любовники, ломовики,
24   Иоанны, Людовики, Ленины,
все это сидело, кряхтя на эх и на ых,
упираясь локтями в колени,
на престолах своих матерых.

34
On Rulers

You will (as sometimes
   people say)
laugh; you will (as clairvoyants
4   say) roar with laughter, gentlemen—
   but, word of honor,
    I have a crony,
     who
8   would be thrilled to shake hands
with the head of a state or of any other
   enterprise.

Since when, I wonder,
12   in the pit of the stomach
we've begun to experience a tender
bubbling, when looking through an opera glass
at the burly one, bristly haired, in the grand box?
16   Since when the concept
of authority has been equated
with the seminal notion of patria?

All sorts of Romans and butchers;
20   Charles the Handsome and Charles the Hideous;
utterly rotten princelings; fat-breasted
German ladies; and various
cannibals, loverboys, lumbermen,
24   Johns, Lewises, Lenins,
emitting stool grunts of strain and release,
   propping elbows on knees,
sat on their massive old thrones.

Умирает со скуки историк:
за Мамаем все тот же Мамай.
В самом деле, нельзя же нам с горя
поступить, как чиновный Китай,
кучу лишних веков присчитавший
к истории скромной своей,
от этого, впрочем, не ставшей
ни лучше, ни веселей.
Кучера государств зато хороши
при исполнении должности: шибко
ледяная навстречу летит синева,
огневые трещат на ветру рукава...
Наблюдатель глядит иностранный
и спереди видит прекрасные очи навыкат,
а сзади прекрасную помесь диванной
подушки с чудовищной тыквой.
Но детина в регалиях или
волк в макинтоше,
в фуражке с немецким крутым козырьком,
охрипший и весь перекошенный,
в остановившемся автомобиле —
или опять же банкет
с кавказским вином —
нет.
Покойный мой тезка,
писавший стихи и в полоску
и в клетку, на самом восходе
всесоюзно-мещанского класса,
кабы дожил до полдня,

28
32
36
40
44
48
52
56

28   The historian dies of sheer boredom:
On the heels of Mamay comes another Mamay.
Does our plight really force us to do
    what did bureaucratic Cathay
32   that with heaps of superfluous centuries
augmented her limited history
(which, however, hardly became
    either better or merrier)?
36   Per contra, the coachmen of empires look good
when performing their duties: swiftly
toward them flies the blue of the sky;
their flame-colored sleeves clap in the wind;
40   the foreign observer looks on and sees
in front bulging eyes of great beauty
and behind a beautiful blend
of divan cushion and monstrous pumpkin.
44   But the decorated big fellow or else
    the trench-coated wolf
    in his army cap with a German steep peak,
    hoarse-voiced, his face all distorted,
48   speaking from an immobile convertible,
or, again, a banquet
with Caucasian wine.
    No, thank you.

52   If my late namesake,
who used to write verse, in rank
and in file, at the very dawn
of the Soviet Small-Bourgeois order,
56   had lived till its noon

нынче бы рифмы натягивал
на «монументален»,
на «переперчил» —
и так далее.

Кембридж (Масс.), 1944

he would be now finding taut rhymes
      such as "praline"
        or "air chill,"
60   and others of the same kind.

Cambridge, Massachusetts, 1944

Notes

Lines 14–15. Tourists attending performances at Soviet theaters used to be deeply impressed by the late dictator's presence.

Line 29/*Mamay*. A particularly evil Tartar prince of the fourteenth century.

Line 35. One recalls Stalin's hilarious pronouncement: "Life has grown better, life has grown merrier!"

Lines 42–43. A humorous description of the generously stuffed behind of a Russian coachman in old Russia.

Lines 44–48. A Soviet general and Adolf Hitler make a brief appearance.

Lines 49–50. Our last stop is at Teheran.

Line 52/*my late namesake*. An allusion to the Christian name and patronymic of Vladimir Vladimirovich Mayakovski (1893–1930), minor Soviet poet, endowed with a certain brilliance and bite, but fatally corrupted by the regime he faithfully served.

Lines 58–59/"praline" . . . "air chill." In the original, *monumentalen*, meaning "[he is] monumental" rhymes pretty closely with *Stalin;* and *pereperchil*, meaning "[he] put in too much pepper," offers an ingenuous correspondence with the name of the British politician in a slovenly Russian pronunciation ("chair-chill").

35
К КН. С. М. КАЧУРИНУ

1

Качурин, твой совет я принял
и вот уж третий день живу
в музейной обстановке, в синей
гостиной с видом на Неву.

Священником американским
твой бедный друг переодет,
и всем долинам дагестанским
я шлю завистливый привет.

От холода, от перебоев
в подложном паспорте, не сплю:
исследователям обоев
лилеи и лианы шлю.

Но спит, на канапе устроясь,
коленки приложив к стене
и завернувшись в плед по пояс,
толмач, приставленный ко мне.

2

Когда я в это воскресенье,
по истечении почти
тридцатилетнего затменья
мог встать и до окна дойти;

Когда увидел я, в тумане
весны и молодого дня

35
To Prince S. M. Kachurin

1

Kachurin, your advice I've accepted
and here I am, living for the third day
in a museumist setup: a blue
4   drawing room with a view on the Neva.

As an American clergyman
your poor friend is disguised,
and to all the Daghestan valleys
8   I send envious greetings.

Because of the cold, and the palpitations
of a false passport, I cannot sleep.
To wallpaper investigators
12   lianas and lilies I send.

But *he* sleeps (curled up on a canapé,
knees snugly pressed to the wall,
in a plaid rug wrapped up to the waist)
16   —the interpreter I've been assigned.

2

When last Sunday,
after the lapse of almost
thirty years of eclipse, I managed
20   to get up and walk as far as the window;

when I saw, in the mist
of spring and of the young day

и заглушенных очертаний,
то, что хранилось у меня

24

так долго, вроде слишком яркой
цветной открытки без угла
(отрезанного ради марки,
которая в углу была);

28

когда все это появилось
так близко от моей души,
она, вздохнув, остановилась,
как поезд в полевой тиши.

32

И за-город мне захотелось:
в истоме юности опять
мечтательно заныло тело,
и начал я соображать,

36

как буду я сидеть в вагоне,
как я его уговорю —
но тут зачмокал он спросонья
и потянулся к словарю.

40

3

На этом я не успокоюсь,
тут объясненье жизни всей,
остановившейся, как поезд
в шершавой тишине полей.

44

Воображаю щебетанье
в шестидесяти девяти
верстах от города, от зданья,
где запинаюсь взаперти,

48

and of muted outlines,
24 all that had been in my keeping

for so long—as a sort of too bright
picture postcard minus one corner
(cut off for the sake of the stamp
28 which had been in that corner);

when it all reappeared
so close to my soul,
my soul, emitting a sigh,
32 stopped like a train in the stillness of fields.

And I yearned to go off to the country:
with the languor of youth once more
my body dreamily ached
36 and I began to consider

how I'd sit in a railway carriage,
how I'd prevail upon him—
but here with slow smacks of lips he woke up
40 and reached for his dictionary.

3

On this I can't rest my case,
here explained is one's entire life
that has stopped like a train
44 in the rough-textured stillness of fields.

I imagine the twitter
at a distance of fifty
miles from the city,
48 from the house where, shut in, I stutter.

и станцию, и дождь наклонный,
на темном видный, и потом
захлест сирени станционной,
уж огрубевшей под дождем,

и дальше: фартук тарантасный
в дрожащих ручейках, и все
подробности берез, и красный
амбар налево от шоссе.

Да, все подробности, Качурин,
все бедненькие, каковы
край сизой тучи, ромб лазури
и крап ствола сквозь рябь листвы.

Но как я сяду в поезд дачный
в таком пальто, в таких очках
(и в сущности совсем прозрачный,
с романом Сирина в руках)?

4

Мне страшно. Ни столбом ростральным,
ни ступенями при луне,
ведущими к огням спиральным,
ко ртутной и тугой волне,

не заслоняется... при встрече
я, впрочем, все скажу тебе
о новом, о широкоплечем
провинциале и рабе.

Мне хочется домой. Довольно.
Качурин, можно мне домой?
В пампасы молодости вольной,

And the station, the slanting rain
seen against a dark background, and then
the petticoat toss of the station lilacs
52   already coarsening under the rain.

Next: the tarantass with its leathern lap cover
crossed by trembling trickles; and all
the details of the birch trees; and the red
56   barn to the left of the highway.

Yes, all the details, Kachurin,
all the poor little ones, such as
edge of dove-gray cloud, lozenge of azure,
60   stipple of tree trunk through ripple of leaves.

But how shall I take the local train,
wearing this coat, wearing these glasses
(and in point of fact completely translucent
64   with a novel of Sirin in my hands)?

4

I'm frightened. Neither the rostral column,
nor the steps that lead, under the moon,
down to the spiral reflections of lights,
68   to the compact quicksilver wave

can mask—— Anyway at our next meeting
I shall tell you everything
about the new, the broadshouldered
72   provincial and slave.

I want to go home. I've had enough.
Kachurin, may I go home?
To the pampas of my free youth,

76   в тексасы, найденные мной.

Я спрашиваю, не пора-ли
вернуться к теме тетивы,
к чарующему «чапаралю»
80   из Всадника без Головы,

чтоб в Матагордовом Ущелье
заснуть на огненных камнях,
с лицом сухим от акварели,
84   с пером вороньим в волосах?

Кембридж (Масс.), 1947

76   to the Texas I once discovered.

I'm asking you: Isn't it time
to return to the theme of the bowstring,
or to what is enchantingly called "chaparral"
80   in *The Headless Horseman*,

so as to fall asleep in Matagordo Gorge,
on the fiery-hot boulders there
with the skin of one's face parched by aquarelle
            paint,
84   and a crow's feather stuck in one's hair?

Cambridge, Massachusetts, 1947

Notes

Line 1/*Kachurin*, Stephan Mstislavovich. Pronounced "Kachoorin" with the accent on the middle syllable. My poor friend, a former White Army colonel, died a few years ago in an Alaskan monastery. The prince's golden heart, moderate brain power, and senile optimism, could alone have been responsible for his suggesting the journey depicted here. His daughter is married to the composer Tornitsen.

Line 7/*Daghestan*. Alludes to Lermontov's famous poem beginning: "At noontime, in a dale of Daghestan."

36
БЫЛ ДЕНЬ КАК ДЕНЬ

Был день как день. Дремала память. Длилась
холодная и скучная весна.
Внезапно тень на дне зашевелилась —
4   и поднялась с рыданием со дна.

О чем рыдать? Утешить не умею —
но как затопала, как затряслась,
как горячо цепляется за шею,
8   в ужасном мраке на руки просясь.

Итака, 1951

36
A Day Like Any Other

A day like any other. Memory dozed. A chilly
and dreary spring dragged on. Then, all at once,
a shadow at the bottom stirred
4   and from the bottom rose with sobs.

What's there to sob about? I'm a poor soother!
Yet how she stamps her feet, and shakes, and hotly
clings to my neck and in the dreadful darkness
8   begs to be gathered up, as babes are, in one's arms.

Ithaca, New York, 1951

37
НЕПРАВИЛЬНЫЕ ЯМБЫ

В последний раз лиясь листами
между воздушными перстами
и проходя перед грозой
от зелени уже назойливой

до серебристости простой,
олива бедная, листва
искусства, плещет, и слова
лелеять бы уже не стоило,

если б не зоркие глаза
и одобрение бродяги,
если б не лилия в овраге,
если б не близкая гроза.

Итака, 1953 г.

37
Irregular Iambics

For the last time, with leaves that flow
between the fingers of the air
and pass before the thunderstorm
from green by now importunate
into a simple silverness,
it ripples, the poor olive: foliage
of art! And it would seem that words
were now no longer worth the fondling,
had there not been a vagabond's
sharp-sightedness and approbation,
had not the gully held its lily,
had not the thunderstorm drawn near.

4

8

12

Ithaca, New York, 1953

Note

Title. "Irregular" (or "faulty," *nepravil'nïe*) refers to the fact that in Russian prosody *ésli* (if) is never scudded, as for example the word *méshdu* (between) is allowed to be by an old tradition. There is no reason, however, why this other light and fluid disyllable should not be treated similarly, especially at the beginning of an iambic line.

38
КАКОЕ СДЕЛАЛ Я ДУРНОЕ ДЕЛО

Какое сделал я дурное дело,
и я ли развратитель и злодей,
я, заставляющий мечтать мир целый
    о бедной девочке моей?

4

О, знаю я, меня боятся люди,
и жгут таких как я за волшебство,
и как от яда в полом изумруде
    мрут от искусства моего.

8

Но как забавно, что в конце абзаца,
корректору и веку вопреки,
тень русской ветки будет колебаться
    на мраморе моей руки.

12

Сан-Ремо, 1959 г.

38
What Is the Evil Deed

What is the evil deed I have committed?
Seducer, criminal—is this the word
for me who set the entire world a-dreaming
    of my poor little girl?

Oh, I know well that I am feared by people:
They burn the likes of me for wizard wiles
and as of poison in a hollow smaragd
    of my art die.

Amusing, though, that at the last indention,
despite proofreaders and my age's ban,
a Russian branch's shadow shall be playing
    upon the marble of my hand.

San Remo, 1959

Note

Lines 1–4. The first strophe imitates the beginning of Boris Pasternak's poem in which he points out that his notorious novel "made the whole world shed tears over the beauty of [his] native land."

39
С СЕРОГО СЕВЕРА

С серого севера
вот пришли эти снимки.

Жизнь успела не все
погасить недоимки.
Знакомое дерево
вырастает из дымки.

Вот на Лугу шоссе.
Дом с колоннами. Оредежь.
Отовсюду почти
мне к себе до сих пор еще
удалось бы пройти.

Так, бывало, купальщикам
на приморском песке
приносится мальчиком
кое-что в кулачке.

Всё, от камушка этого
с каймой фиолетовой
до стеклышка матово-
зеленоватого,
он приносит торжественно.

Вот это Батово.
Вот это Рожествено.

Монтрё, 1967 г.

39
From the Gray North

From the gray North
now come these photos.

Not all its arrears
4   life has had time to defray.
A familiar tree reappears
out of the gray.

This is the highway to Luga.
8   My house with the pillars. The Oredezh.
Almost from anywhere
homeward even today
I can still find my way.

12   Thus, sometimes, to the bathers
on the seaside sand
a small boy will bring over
something in his clenched hand.

16   Everything—from a pebble
with a violet rim
to the dim greenish part of a
glass object—is festively
20   brought over by him.

This is Batovo.
This is Rozhestveno.

Montreux, 1967

FOURTEEN ENGLISH POEMS

A Literary Dinner

Come here, said my hostess, her face making room
for one of those pink introductory smiles
that link, like a valley of fruit trees in bloom,
the slopes of two names.
I want you, she murmured, to eat Dr. James.

I was hungry. The Doctor looked good. He had read
the great book of the week and had liked it, he said,
because it was powerful. So I was brought
a generous helping. His mauve-bosomed wife
kept showing me, very politely, I thought,
the tenderest bits with the point of her knife.
I ate—and in Egypt the sunsets were swell;
The Russians were doing remarkably well;
had I met a Prince Poprinsky, whom he had known
in Caparabella, or was it Mentone?
They had traveled extensively, he and his wife;
her hobby was People, his hobby was Life.
All was good and well cooked, but the tastiest part
was his nut-flavored, crisp cerebellum. The heart
resembled a shiny brown date,
and I stowed all the studs on the edge of my plate.

1942

The Refrigerator Awakes

Crash!
And if darkness could sound, it would sound like this giant
waking up in the torture house, trying to die
and not dying, and trying
not to cry and immediately crying
that he will, that he will, that he will do his best
to adjust his dark soul to the pressing request
of the only true frost,
and he pants and he gasps and he rasps and he wheezes:
ice is the solid form when the water freezes;
a volatile liquid (see "Refrigerating")
is permitted to pass into evaporating
coils, where it boils,
which somehow seems wrong,
and I wonder how long
it will rumble and shudder and crackle and pound;
Scudder, the Alpinist, slipped and was found
half a century later preserved in blue ice
with his bride and two guides and a dead edelweiss;
a German has proved that the snowflakes we see
are the germ cells of stars and the sea life to be;
hold
the line, hold the line, lest its tale be untold;
let it amble along through the thumping pain
and horror of dichlordisomethingmethane,
a trembling white heart with the frost froth upon it,
Nova Zembla, poor thing, with that B in her bonnet,
stunned bees in the bonnets of cars on hot roads,
Keep it Kold, says a poster in passing, and lo,
loads,

of bright fruit, and a ham, and some chocolate cream,
and three bottles of milk, all contained in the gleam
of that wide-open white
god, the pride and delight
of starry-eyed couples in dream kitchenettes,
and it groans and it drones and it toils and it sweats—
Shackleton, pemmican, penguin, Poe's Pym—
collapsing at last in the criminal
night.

1942

3
A Discovery

I found it in a legendary land
all rocks and lavender and tufted grass,
where it was settled on some sodden sand
hard by the torrent of a mountain pass.

The features it combines mark it as new
to science: shape and shade—the special tinge,
akin to moonlight, tempering its blue,
the dingy underside, the checquered fringe.

My needles have teased out its sculptured sex;
corroded tissues could no longer hide
that priceless mote now dimpling the convex
and limpid teardrop on a lighted slide.

Smoothly a screw is turned; out of the mist
two ambered hooks symmetrically slope,
or scales like battledores of amethyst
cross the charmed circle of the microscope.

I found it and I named it, being versed
in taxonomic Latin; thus became
godfather to an insect and its first
describer—and I want no other fame.

Wide open on its pin (though fast asleep),
and safe from creeping relatives and rust,
in the secluded stronghold where we keep
type specimens it will transcend its dust.

Dark pictures, thrones, the stones that pilgrims kiss,
poems that take a thousand years to die
but ape the immortality of this
red label on a little butterfly.

1943

4
The Poem

Not the sunset poem you make when you think
       aloud,
with its linden tree in India ink
and the telegraph wires across its pink
       cloud;

not the mirror in you and her delicate bare
shoulder still glimmering there;
not the lyrical click of a pocket rhyme—
the tiny music that tells the time;

and not the pennies and weights on those
evening papers piled up in the rain;
not the cacodemons of carnal pain;
not the things you can say so much better in plain
   prose—

but the poem that hurtles from heights unknown
—when you wait for the splash of the stone
deep below, and grope for your pen,
and then comes the shiver, and then—

in the tangle of sounds, the leopards of words,
the leaflike insects, the eye-spotted birds
fuse and form a silent, intense,
mimetic pattern of perfect sense.

1944

5
An Evening of Russian Poetry

*". . . seems to be the best train. Miss Ethel Winter
of the Department of English will meet you at the
station and . . ."*

FROM A LETTER ADDRESSED TO THE VISITING SPEAKER

The subject chosen for tonight's discussion
is everywhere, though often incomplete:
when their basaltic banks become too steep,
most rivers use a kind of rapid Russian,
and so do children talking in their sleep.
My little helper at the magic lantern,
insert that slide and let the colored beam
project my name or any such-like phantom
in Slavic characters upon the screen.
The other way, the other way. I thank you.

On mellow hills the Greek, as you remember,
fashioned his alphabet from cranes in flight;
his arrows crossed the sunset, then the night.
Our simple skyline and a taste for timber,
the influence of hives and conifers,
reshaped the arrows and the borrowed birds.
Yes, Sylvia?

> *"Why do you speak of words
> when all we want is knowledge nicely browned?"*

Because all hangs together—shape and sound,
heather and honey, vessel and content.
Not only rainbows—every line is bent,
and skulls and seeds and all good worlds are round,

like Russian verse, like our colossal vowels:
those painted eggs, those glossy pitcher flowers
that swallow whole a golden bumblebee,
those shells that hold a thimble and the sea.
Next question.

"Is your prosody like ours?"

Well, Emmy, our pentameter may seem
to foreign ears as if it could not rouse
the limp iambus from its pyrrhic dream.
But close your eyes and listen to the line.
The melody unwinds; the middle word
is marvelously long and serpentine:
you hear one beat, but you have also heard
the shadow of another, then the third
touches the gong, and then the fourth one sighs.

It makes a very fascinating noise:
it opens slowly, like a greyish rose
in pedagogic films of long ago.

The rhyme is the line's birthday, as you know,
and there are certain customary twins
in Russian as in other tongues. For instance,
love automatically rhymes with blood,
nature with liberty, sadness with distance,
humane with everlasting, prince with mud,
moon with a multitude of words, but sun
and song and wind and life and death with none.

Beyond the seas where I have lost a scepter,
I hear the neighing of my dappled nouns,
soft participles coming down the steps,

treading on leaves, trailing their rustling gowns,
and liquid verbs in *ahla* and in *ili*,
Aonian grottoes, nights in the Altai,
black pools of sound with "l"s for water lilies.
The empty glass I touched is tinkling still,
but now 'tis covered by a hand and dies.

"Trees? Animals? Your favorite precious stone?"

The birch tree, Cynthia, the fir tree, Joan.
Like a small caterpillar on its thread,
my heart keeps dangling from a leaf long dead
but hanging still, and still I see the slender
white birch that stands on tiptoe in the wind,
and firs beginning where the garden ends,
the evening ember glowing through their cinders.

Among the animals that haunt our verse,
that bird of bards, regale of night, comes first:
scores of locutions mimicking its throat
render its every whistling, bubbling, bursting,
flutelike or cuckoolike or ghostlike note.
But lapidary epithets are few;
we do not deal in universal rubies.
The angle and the glitter are subdued;
our riches lie concealed. We never liked
the jeweler's window in the rainy night.

My back is Argus-eyed. I live in danger.
False shadows turn to track me as I pass
and, wearing beards, disguised as secret agents,
creep in to blot the freshly written page
and read the blotter in the looking glass.

And in the dark, under my bedroom window,
until, with a chill whirr and shiver, day
presses its starter, warily they linger
or silently approach the door and ring
the bell of memory and run away.

Let me allude, before the spell is broken,
to Pushkin, rocking in his coach on long
and lonely roads: he dozed, then he awoke,
undid the collar of his traveling cloak,
and yawned, and listened to the driver's song.
Amorphous sallow bushes called *rakeety*,
enormous clouds above an endless plain,
songline and skyline endlessly repeated,
the smell of grass and leather in the rain.
And then the sob, the syncope (Nekrasov!),
the panting syllables that climb and climb,
obsessively repetitive and rasping,
dearer to some than any other rhyme.
And lovers meeting in a tangled garden,
dreaming of mankind, of untrammeled life,
mingling their longings in the moonlit garden,
where trees and hearts are larger than in life.
This passion for expansion you may follow
throughout our poetry. We want the mole
to be a lynx or turn into a swallow
by some sublime mutation of the soul.
But to unneeded symbols consecrated,
escorted by a vaguely infantile
path for bare feet, our roads were always fated
to lead into the silence of exile.

Had I more time tonight I would unfold

the whole amazing story—*neighuklúzhe,*
nevynossímo—but I have to go.

What did I say under my breath? I spoke
to a blind songbird hidden in a hat,
safe from my thumbs and from the eggs I broke
into the gibus brimming with their yolk.

And now I must remind you in conclusion,
that I am followed everywhere and that
space is collapsible, although the bounty
of memory is often incomplete:
once in a dusty place in Mora county
(half town, half desert, dump mound and mesquite)
and once in West Virginia (a muddy
red road between an orchard and a veil
of tepid rain) it came, that sudden shudder,
a Russian something that I could inhale
but could not see. Some rapid words were uttered—
and then the child slept on, the door was shut.

The conjurer collects his poor belongings—
the colored handkerchief, the magic rope,
the double-bottomed rhymes, the cage, the song.
You tell him of the passes you detected.
The mystery remains intact. The check
comes forward in its smiling envelope.

"How would you say 'delightful talk' in Russian?"
"How would you say 'good night'?"

                                    Oh, that would be:

Bessónnitza, tvoy vzor oonýl i stráshen;
lubóv moyá, otstóopnika prostée.

(Insomnia, your stare is dull and ashen,
my love, forgive me this apostasy.)

1945

6
The Room

The room a dying poet took
at nightfall in a dead hotel
had both directories—the Book
of Heaven and the Book of Bell.

It had a mirror and a chair,
it had a window and a bed,
its ribs let in the darkness where
rain glistened and a shopsign bled.

Not tears, not terror, but a blend
of anonymity and doom,
it seemed, that room, to condescend
to imitate a normal room.

Whenever some automobile
subliminally slit the night,
the walls and ceiling would reveal
a wheeling skeleton of light.

Soon afterwards the room was mine.
A similar striped cageling, I
groped for the lamp and found the line
"Alone, unknown, unloved, I die"

in pencil, just above the bed.
It had a false quotation air.
Was it a she, wild-eyed, well-read,
or a fat man with thinning hair?

I asked a gentle Negro maid,
I asked a captain and his crew,
I asked the night clerk. Undismayed,
I asked a drunk. Nobody knew.

Perhaps when he had found the switch
he saw the picture on the wall
and cursed the red eruption which
tried to be maples in the fall?

Artistically in the style
of Mr. Churchill at his best,
those maples marched in double file
from Glen Lake to Restricted Rest.

Perhaps my text is incomplete.
A poet's death is, after all,
a question of technique, a neat
enjambment, a melodic fall.

And here a life had come apart
in darkness, and the room had grown
a ghostly thorax, with a heart
unknown, unloved—but not alone.

1950

7
Voluptates Tactionum

Some inevitable day
On the editorial page
Of your paper it will say,
"Tactio has come of age."

When you turn a knob, your set
Will obligingly exhale
Forms, invisible and yet
Tangible—a world in Braille.

Think of all the things that will
Really be within your reach!
Phantom bottle, dummy pill,
Limpid limbs upon a beach.

Grouped before a Magnotact,
Clubs and families will clutch
Everywhere the same compact
Paradise (in terms of touch).

Palpitating fingertips
Will caress the flossy hair
And investigate the lips
Simulated in midair.

See the schoolboy, like a blind
Lover, frantically grope
For the shape of love—and find
Nothing but the shape of soap.

1951

8
Restoration

To think that any fool may tear
by chance the web of when and where.
O window in the dark! To think
that every brain is on the brink
of nameless bliss no brain can bear,

unless there be no great surprise—
as when you learn to levitate
and, hardly trying, realize
—alone, in a bright room—that weight
is but your shadow, and you rise.

My little daughter wakes in tears:
She fancies that her bed is drawn
into a dimness which appears
to be the deep of all her fears
but which, in point of fact, is dawn.

I know a poet who can strip
a William Tell or Golden Pip
in one uninterrupted peel
miraculously to reveal,
revolving on his fingertip,

a snowball. So I would unrobe,
turn inside out, pry open, probe
all matter, everything you see,
the skyline and its saddest tree,
the whole inexplicable globe,

to find the true, the ardent core
as doctors of old pictures do
when, rubbing out a distant door
or sooty curtain, they restore
the jewel of a bluish view.

1952

9
The Poplar

Before this house a poplar grows
Well versed in dowsing, I suppose,

But how it sighs! And every night
A boy in black, a girl in white

Beyond the brightness of my bed
Appear, and not a word is said.

On coated chair and coatless chair
They sit, one here, the other there.

I do not care to make a scene:
I read a glossy magazine.

He props upon his slender knee
A dwarfed and potted poplar tree.

And she—she seems to hold a dim
Hand mirror with an ivory rim

Framing a lawn, and her, and me
Under the prototypic tree,

Before a pillared porch, last seen
In July, nineteen seventeen.

This is the silver lining of
Pathetic fallacies: the sough

Of *Populus* that taps at last
Not water but the author's past.

And note: nothing is ever said.
I read a magazine in bed

Or the *Home Book of Verse;* and note:
This is my shirt, that is my coat.

But frailer seers I am told
Get up to rearrange a fold.

1952

10

Lines Written in Oregon

Esmeralda! Now we rest
Here, in the bewitched and blest
Mountain forests of the West.

Here the very air is stranger.
Damzel, anchoret, and ranger
Share the woodland's dream and danger.

And to think I deemed you dead!
(In a dungeon, it was said;
Tortured, strangled); but instead—

Blue birds from the bluest fable,
Bear and hare in coats of sable,
Peacock moth on picnic table.

Huddled roadsigns softly speak
Of Lake Merlin, Castle Creek,
And (obliterated) Peak.

Do you recognize that clover?
Dandelions, *l'or du pauvre?*
(Europe, nonetheless, is over).

Up the turf, along the burn,
Latin lilies climb and turn
Into Gothic fir and fern.

Cornfields have befouled the prairies
But these canyons laugh! And there is
Still the forest with its fairies.

And I rest where I awoke
In the sea shade—*l'ombre glauque*—
Of a legendary oak;

Where the woods get ever dimmer,
Where the Phantom Orchids glimmer—
Esmeralda, *immer, immer*.

1953

11

Ode to a Model

I have followed you, model,
in magazine ads through all seasons,
from dead leaf on the sod
to red leaf on the breeze,

from your lily-white armpit
to the tip of your butterfly eyelash,
charming and pitiful,
silly and stylish.

Or in kneesocks and tartan
standing there like some fabulous symbol,
parted feet pointing outward
—pedal form of akimbo.

On a lawn, in a parody
Of Spring and its cherry tree,
near a vase and a parapet,
virgin practicing archery.

Ballerina, black-masked,
near a parapet of alabaster.
"Can one—somebody asked—
rhyme 'star' and 'disaster'?"

Can one picture a blackbird
as the negative of a small firebird?
Can a record, run backward,
turn 'repaid' into 'diaper'?

Can one marry a model?
Kill your past, make you real, raise a family,
by removing you bodily
from back numbers of Sham?

1955

12

On Translating "Eugene Onegin"

1

What is translation? On a platter
A poet's pale and glaring head,
A parrot's screech, a monkey's chatter,
And profanation of the dead.
The parasites you were so hard on
Are pardoned if I have your pardon,
O, Pushkin, for my stratagem:
I traveled down your secret stem,
And reached the root, and fed upon it;
Then, in a language newly learned,
I grew another stalk and turned
Your stanza patterned on a sonnet,
Into my honest roadside prose—
All thorn, but cousin to your rose.

2

Reflected words can only shiver
Like elongated lights that twist
In the black mirror of a river
Between the city and the mist.
Elusive Pushkin! Persevering,
I still pick up Tatiana's earring,
Still travel with your sullen rake.
I find another man's mistake,
I analyze alliterations
That grace your feasts and haunt the great
Fourth stanza of your Canto Eight.
This is my task—a poet's patience
And scholiastic passion blent:
Dove-droppings on your monument.

1955

13
Rain

How mobile is the bed on these
nights of gesticulating trees
    when the rain clatters fast,
the tin-toy rain with dapper hoof
trotting upon an endless roof,
    traveling into the past.

Upon old roads the steeds of rain
Slip and slow down and speed again
    through many a tangled year;
but they can never reach the last
dip at the bottom of the past
    because the sun is there.

1956

The Ballad of Longwood Glen

That Sunday morning, at half past ten,
Two cars crossed the creek and entered the glen.

In the first was Art Longwood, a local florist,
With his children and wife (now Mrs. Deforest).

In the one that followed, a ranger saw
Art's father, stepfather and father-in-law.

The three old men walked off to the cove.
Through tinkling weeds Art slowly drove.

Fair was the morning, with bright clouds afar.
Children and comics emerged from the car.

Silent Art, who could stare at a thing all day,
Watched a bug climb a stalk and fly away.

Pauline had asthma, Paul used a crutch.
They were cute little rascals but could not run much.

"I wish," said his mother to crippled Paul,
"Some man would teach you to pitch that ball."

Silent Art took the ball and tossed it high.
It stuck in a tree that was passing by.

And the grave green pilgrim turned and stopped.
The children waited, but no ball dropped.

"I never climbed trees in my timid prime,"
Thought Art; and forthwith started to climb.

Now and then his elbow or knee could be seen
In a jigsaw puzzle of blue and green.

Up and up Art Longwood swarmed and shinned,
And the leaves said *yes* to the questioning wind.

What tiaras of gardens! What torrents of light!
How accessible ether! How easy flight!

His family circled the tree all day.
Pauline concluded: "Dad climbed away."

None saw the delirious celestial crowds
Greet the hero from earth in the snow of the clouds.

Mrs. Longwood was getting a little concerned.
He never came down. He never returned.

She found some change at the foot of the tree.
The children grew bored. Paul was stung by a bee.

The old men walked over and stood looking up,
Each holding five cards and a paper cup.

Cars on the highway stopped, backed, and then
Up a rutted road waddled into the glen.

And the tree was suddenly full of noise,
Conventioners, fishermen, freckled boys.

Anacondas and pumas were mentioned by some,
And all kinds of humans continued to come:

Tree surgeons, detectives, the fire brigade.
An ambulance parked in the dancing shade.

A drunken rogue with a rope and a gun
Arrived on the scene to see justice done.

Explorers, dendrologists—all were there;
And a strange pale girl with gypsy hair.

And from Cape Fear to Cape Flattery
Every paper had: Man Lost in Tree.

And the sky-bound oak (where owls had perched
And the moon dripped gold) was felled and searched.

They discovered some inchworms, a red-cheeked gall,
And an ancient nest with a new-laid ball.

They varnished the stump, put up railings and signs.
Restrooms nestled in roses and vines.

Mrs. Longwood, retouched, when the children died,
Became a photographer's dreamy bride.

And now the Deforests, with *four* old men,
Like regular tourists visit the glen;

Munch their lunches, look up and down,
Wash their hands, and drive back to town.

1957

EIGHTEEN CHESS PROBLEMS

V. Nabokov (U.S.A.)

1

Mate in two moves

Composed in Paris, mid-May 1940 (a few days before mi-grating to America). Published in *Speak, Memory*, 1951, and included by Lipton, Matthews, and Rice in *Chess Problems*, London, 1963. The irresistible try is for the bafflement of sophisticated solvers.

For solutions to the chess problems, turn to page 201.

2

Mate in three moves

In this miniature (composed in Montreux, Switzerland, March 1, 1965) a rather blunt key is redeemed by the variations and tries. The two model mates, rank and file, echo each other. The problem is not quite as easy as it seems at first blush.

3

Mate in two moves

The key deceptively prevents the set mate B x Pe4 after
P to f4. The interest of this problem (composed in Mon-
treux, March 22, 1965, and published in *The Trinity Review*,
Cambridge, England, Lent 1969) lies in the three main vari-
ations with the B advancing one spasmodic step every time.

4

Mate in three moves

The point of this problem (Montreux, April 10, 1965; published in *The Sunday Times*, London, December 29, 1968) consists in that Black's R clears the way for White's mating piece by capturing an intervening whitey, so that when it (Black's R) returns to its initial square, it can be captured with mate. This is the so-called "Nabokov Theme."

5

Mate in two moves

Composed in Montreux, April 20, 1965. The key changes the
set play (after Black's P moves). There are some good tries.
Note that the tempting discovered check on the fifth rank
never materializes.

6

Mate in three moves

The key is deceptive, because it seems to interfere with the Q's possible use of the square it involves; and, anyway, other eighth-rank squares look more plausible. The main idea of this elegant problem (composed at the Grande Albergo Excelsior, Ponte di Legno, North Italy, on July 18, 1966, a rainy break in some strenuous butterfly hunting, and published in *The Sunday Times*, London, November 5, 1967) lies in the Black K's clearing the way to his doom by eliminating a white man. All in all, my most satisfying three-mover.

7

Mate in three moves

The subtle key spoils the set play after 1 . . . K–h4. Nice tries. The problem was composed in Montreux, October 1, 1966, and published in *The Problemist*, November 1969. It was placed third with a Second Prize in that journal's Intermediate Composing Tourney.

8

Mate in three moves

The Kt's attacking the Q, less to take it than to bring it back eventually to its original square from wherever it moves to, with mate by another piece, represents an idea that struck me as new at the time of composing this problem (Montreux, October 22, 1966).

9

Mate in three moves

Composed at the Cenobio dei Dogi, Camogli, near Genoa, April 15, 1967, entomologically disappointing; and published in the *Evening News*, London, October 14, 1967. The main idea of this slightly old-fashioned miniature is the White Kt's return to its initial square in the main variation.

10

Mate in two moves

Camogli, June 8, 1967. The presence of the B on a1 is a bit
of not quite legal camouflage allowing the set play 1, . . .
P d4–d3 etc., a possibility diverting the solver's attention
from the key, which *prevents* P d4–d3. The position of the
B on f5 (guarding the escape to d7 after 1 . . . Kc6) pro-
vides another set mate which is changed by the key.

11

Mate in three moves

The prevention of duals after Black's B and P moves is one of the themes of this amusing problem composed in the gardens of the Palace Hotel, Montreux, August 13, 1967, and published in *The Problemist*, November 1970.

Best try: 1 Kt–e6 K–h3 2 Kt–f4 K:P? 3 R–h5 mate

12

Mate in three moves

A neat but rather pallid waiter. Composed in Montreux,
September 3, 1968.

13

Mate in two moves

A self-interference freak not for the conservative solver. It was composed in Montreux, on October 3, 1968 (in the afterglow of completed *Ada*), and published in the *Evening News*, London, December 24, 1968.

14

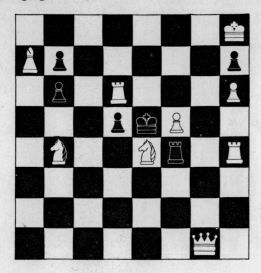

Mate in two moves

Montreux, November 22, 1968. A tricky problem with some good tries. The avoidance of duals, which marks all my compositions, made this one especially difficult and interesting to construct. Published in *The Sunday Times*, February 22, 1970.

15

Mate in three moves

Composed on the last day of 1968, in Montreux, and published in *The Problemist*, November 1969. The eyespot of this colorful problem is the alternative prevention of duals after Black's Kt takes Pe3 or Pg3.

16

Mate in two moves

The key changes the set mate Kt–b6 after B–e8. This seems to be my most ingenious two-mover. It was composed in Montreux, February 13, 1969, and appeared in *The Problemist*, January 1970.

17

Mate in three moves

This problem, composed in Montreux, August 8, 1970, and published in *The Problemist*, November 1970, features a curious case of self-block (allowing the unpinning of Black's Kt), as well as zugzwang in the second variation and an additional pin in the third.

18

White retracts its last move and mates in one

I dedicated this fairy to the great Russian player Evgeniy Znosko-Borovski on the occasion of his twenty-fifth anniversary of champion chess. He published it in the chess column of the *émigré* daily *Poslednie novosti*, Paris, November 17, 1932. It is signed "V. Sirin," the main pen name I used in those years. Republished in the *New Statesman*, London, December 12, 1969.

SOLUTIONS

I

White: Ka7, Qb6, Rf4, h5, Be4, h8, Ktd8, e6, Pb7, g3
Black: Ke5, Rg7, Bh6, Kte2, g5, Pc3, c6, d7
Mate in two moves
Key: Be4–c2

1 . . . K–d5 (or d6)	2 Q–c5 mate
1 . . . P–c5 (or –d6)	2 R–f5 mate
1 . . . P–d5	2 Q–c7 mate
1 . . . Kt any	2 Q–d4 mate

The try Pb8 = Kt, with some good virtual play, is defeated only by P–c2!

2

White: Ke1, Qh2, Ra1, Pe5, g2
Black: Ka8, Pa3
Mate in three moves
Key: Q–h7

1 . . . K–b8, 2 R × P! (*not* R–d1? defeated by K–c8!);
  K–c8 3 R–a8 mate
1 . . . P–a2 2 Q–b1! (*not* R–d1? defeated by P =
  Q pinning the R); K–a7 3 R × P mate.

3

White: Kg8, Qb7, Ra5,h8, Bh7, Ktg5, Pg7,h3
Black: Kh6, Rh5, Ktd6, Pe4, f5, f6, f7, h4
Mate in two moves
Key: QxPe4

1 . . . P–f4	2 B–g6 mate
1 . . . RxKt	2 BxP mate
1 . . . PxQ	2 BxP mate
1 . . . KtxQ	2 KtxP mate
1 . . . KxKt	2 Q–e3 mate

4

White: Ke8, Qh2, Bd4, Ktc2, P d3, d5, e2, f5, h4
Black: Kf4, Rh6, Ktg3, Pd6, e3, f6, g4, h7
Mate in three moves
Key: K–f7

1 . . . R $\times$ P 2 K $\times$ P; R–h6 ch 3 Q $\times$ R mate
1 . . . K $\times$ P 2 Kt $\times$ P ch; K–f4 3 Q–f2 mate
1 . . . any 2 K–e6; any 3 B $\times$ Pe3 mate
Best try: 1 Kt $\times$ P; R $\times$ P 2 Q $\times$ R; P–h5!

5

White: Kh7, Qb1, Rb8, h5, Ba7, b5, Ktta2, Pd4, d7
Black: Ka5, Rc4, Bb4, Pb7
Mate in two moves
Key: R–a8

1 . . . P–b6	2 B–b8 mate
1 . . . B any	2 B–c5 mate
1 . . . R $\times$ P	2 B $\times$ R mate
1 . . . R any other	2 Q $\times$ B mate

6

White: Ka4, Qh2, Ra8, Ktc3, Pc4, d3
Black: Kd4, Pa5, c5, c6
Mate in three moves
Key: R–h8

1 . . . K × Kt	2 R–h3; K–d4	3 Q–b2 mate
1 . . . K × P	2 R–h3 ch; K–d4 (or × P)	3 Q–f4 mate
1 . . . K to e3	2 R–h3 ch; K–d4	3 Kt–e2 mate

Good tries (e.g., 1 K–b3; P–a4 ch 2 K–c2; P–a3 3 Q–f4 mate)

7

White: Kh1, Rg3, g7, Be5, Pe4, h2
Black: Kg5, Pg4, g6, h5
Mate in three moves
Key: P–h3

1 . . . K–h6	2 P–h4; Pg5	3 P × P mate
1 . . . K–h4	2 R × P; P × P	3 B–f6 mate
1 . . . P–h4	2 R–h7; P × R	3 P–h4 mate

A good planted try is 1 K–g1 (*not* -g2 because of Black's second move, an added nicety); K–h6 2 P–h4; P × P en passant 3 R × P g6 mate (all this defeated by 1 . . . P–h4!).

8

White: Kg7, Ba1, Ktd5, h6, P g3
Black: Kg5, Qe4, Pc3, f6, f7, g6, h5
Mate in three moves
Key: Kt × Pc3

1 ... Q any	2 Kt–e4 ch; Q × Kt	3 B × P mate
1 ... P–f5	2 Kt × Q ch; P × Kt	3 B–f6 mate
1 ... P–h4	2 Kt × Q ch; K–h5	3 P–g4 mate

9

White: Kf8, Rc1, Ktf6, f7, Pd2, e4
Black: Kd4, Pd3, d5
Mate in three moves
Key: Kt–d7

1 ... K × P	2 R–f1; P–d4	3 Kt–f6 mate
1 ...	2 ... ; K–d4	3 R–f4 mate
1 ... P × P	2 Kt–b6; P–e3	3 R–c4 mate

A pleasing try is 1 Kt–h6; P × P?
2 Kth6–g4; P–e 3 P × P mate

10

White: Kf7, Qc1, Rb8, Ba1, f5, Ktc4
Black: Kd5, Pc7, d4, d6
Mate in two moves
Key: B–d3

1 ... K–c5	2 Kt–e3 mate
1 ... K–c6	2 Kt–b6! mate
1 ... P–c6	2 Q–g5 mate
1 ... P–c5	2 Q–h1 mate

11

White: Kc3, Re5, Bf2,f7, Ktg5, Ph2
Black: Kg4, Ba6, Kta1, Pb7, c4,f3
Mate in three moves
Key: K–d4

1 . . . K–f4	2 Kt–h3ch; K–g4	3 B–e6 mate
1 . . . Kt–b3ch	2 K–e3; any	3 P mate
1 . . . Kt–c2ch	2 K–e4; any	3 P mate
1 . . . any other	2 Pch; K–f4	3 Kt–e6 mate

12

White: Kg3, Bd7, g7, Ktf5, h4, Pe4, f2, g4, h2, h7
Black: Kf7, Kth8, Pe5, h6
Mate in three moves
Key: P–h3

1 . . . Kt–g6	2 Kt–f3;	Kt	3 Kt f3 × P mate
		P–h5	3 Kt–g5 mate
1 . . . P–h5	2 P × P; Kt–g6		3 P × Kt mate

13

White: Kh4, Qc3, Rd1, g7, Ba2, h2, Kte6, g8
Black: Kf5, Qc6, Rd4, d8, Ba3, a6, Ktc7, f7, Pb7, e4, f6, g4
Mate in two moves
Key: Q–a5 ch

Main variations:

1 . . . Q–b5	2 R–f1 mate
1 . . . Q–c5	2 Kt–e7 mate
1 . . . Q–d5	2 Kt × Rd4 mate

Tries: R × P (defeated by Ktf7–g5), Q–g3 (met by Pe4–e3), and Q × R (countered by Q–c3)

14

White: Kh8, Qg1, Rd6, h4, Ba7, Ktb4, e4, Pf5, h6
Black: Ke5, Rf4, Pb6, b7, d5, h7
Mate in two moves
Key: Q–f2

1 . . . R–f3 (or × Q)	2 R × Pd5 mate
1 . . . R–g4 (or × R or × Kt)	2 R–e6 mate
1 . . . R × P	2 Kt–d3 mate
1 . . . any other	2 Q × R mate

15

White: Kc2, Re1, g6, Ba7, e4, Kth1, P b2, d2, e3, g3
Black: Kg1, Ktf1, P c3, e5, g7, h2
Mate in three moves
Key: R–b1

1 . . . P × Pd2	2 K–d1; Kt any 3 K × P
1 . . . P × Pb2, then:	2 K–d1 with three variations:
2 . . . Kt × Pd2	3 K × Kt
2 . . . Kt × Pe3	3 K–e2 (square c2 closed)
2 . . . Kt × Pg3	3 K–c2 (square e2 closed)

Tries: d2–d4; e5 × d4 ?
etc., and Be4–d3; e5–e4 ?

16
White: Kc4, Q d1, R a8, h8, B b8, Kt d5, g7, P b5
Black: Kd7, Bf7, Pb7, e7
Mate in two moves
Key: Q–h5

1 . . . B–e8   2 Q × B mate

The best tries are b5–b6, B–c7, and Kt–e6

17
White: Kh7, Rh8, Bc8, Kta4, Pc4,d5,e6
Black: Ka6, Bb6, Ktb7, Pa5,a7,c5,d6,d7
Mate in three moves
Key: R–d8

1 . . . B × R   2 B × P; any   3 B mate
1 . . . B–c7   2 R × P; any   3 B × Kt mate
1 . . . P × P   2 R × P; any   3 Kt × P mate

18
White: Kf5, Qf8, Rc7, c8
Black: Kd6, Qb8, Re7, e8, Pd5
White retracts its last move and mates in one

White's P d7 had captured Black's Kt on c8 and made a
Rook; instead of which, P d7 now takes Black's R e8 and
mates with a promoted Knight.

There is some mild magic in the retrospective transforma-
tion of White R into Black Kt, and Black R into White Kt,
with the symmetry of pieces (and White's defense of c7)
retained.

BIBLIOGRAPHY

Russian and English poems

I. Russian poems

1. The Rain Has Flown
   (*Dozhd' proletel*)

   Vyra (North Russia), May, 1917
   Publ. *Almanakh "Dva Puti,"*
   Petrograd, Jan., 1918

2. To Liberty
   (*K Svobode*)

   Gaspra (Crimea), 3/16 Dec.,
   1917

3. I Still Keep Mute
   (*Eshchyo bezmolvstvuyu*)

   Livadia (Crimea), April 4, 1919
   Publ. *Gorniy Put'* (collection of
   verse), Berlin, 1923

4. Hotel Room
   (*Nomer v gostinitse*)

   Hotel Metropole, room 7, Se-
   bastopol, April 8, 1919 (a few
   days before leaving Russia)

5. Provence
   (*Solntse: Slonyayus'
   pereulkami*)

   Solliès-Pont (Var), Aug. 19, 1923
   Publ. *Rul'* (*émigré* daily), Berlin,
   Sept. 1, 1923; reprinted: Prof. E.
   A. Lyatski, *Russian Grammar*,
   Prague, 1927; and *Vozvrashchenie
   Chorba* (collection of stories and
   verse), Berlin, 1930

6. La Bonne Lorraine

   Publ. *Rul'*, Sept. 16, 1924; and
   Vozv. Chorba, Berlin, 1930

7. The Blazon
   (*Gerb*)

   Berlin, Jan. 24, 1925
   Publ. *Russkoe Eho* (a Berlin
   émigré weekly), March 3, 1925

8. The Mother
   (*Mat'*)

   Publ. *Rul'*, April 4, 1925
   and *Russkoe Eho*, same date;
   reprinted *Vozv. Chorba*, Berlin,
   1930

30. Oculus	Unpublished
31. Fame (*Slava*)	Wellesley, Mass., 1942 *Novïy zhurnal* (*émigré* review), New York, 1942; reprinted as above
32. The Paris Poem (*Parizhskaya poema*)	Cambridge, Mass., 1943 *Novïy zhurnal*, 1944; reprinted as above
33. No Matter How (*Kakim bï*)	Cambridge, Mass., early 1944 Publ. in *Stihotvoreniya*, 1952, and *Poesie*, 1962, with Italian version; reprinted in *Modern Russian Poetry*, ed. Markov, 1966, with English version by V. N.
34. On Rulers (*O pravitelyah*)	Cambridge, Mass., 1944. Publ. *Novïy zhurnal*, X, (*émigré* review) New York, 1945; re- printed in 1952 and 1962 colls.
35. To Prince S. M. Kachurin (*Kn. S. M. Kachurinu*)	Cambridge, Mass., early 1947 Publ. *N. Zh.* XV, 1947; reprinted as above
36. A Day Like Any Other (*Bïl den' kak den'*)	Ithaca, N. Y., 1951 Publ. in *Stihotvoreniya*, 1952, and *Poesie*, 1962, with Italian version
37. Irregular Iambics (*Nepravil'nïe yambï*)	Ithaca, N. Y., 1953 Publ. *Opïtï*, I (*émigré* review), New York, 1953 (with misprint, 1.4)
38. What Is the Evil Deed (*Kakoe sdelal ya durnoe delo*)	San Remo (Italy), Dec. 27, 1959 Publ. in *Vozdushnïe puti*, II, (*émigré* review), N. Y., 1961; reprinted in *Modern Russian Poetry*, ed. Markov, 1966, with English version by V. N.
39. From the Gray North (*S Serogo Severa*)	Montreux, Dec. 20, 1967 Publ., facsimile, *Novoe Russkoe Slovo* (*émigré* daily), New York, Jan. 21, 1968

English poems

1. A Literary Dinner   *The New Yorker*, April 11, 1942
Reprinted: *Poems*, New York,
1959 and London, 1961; *Poesie*,
Milano, 1962, with Italian version
by Enzo Siciliano; *Nabokov's
Congeries*, N. Y., 1968

2. The Refrigerator Awakes   *The New Yorker*, June 6, 1942
Reprinted as above

3. A Discovery   *The New Yorker*, May 15, 1943
Reprinted as above. Also reprinted
in *The New Yorker Book of
Poems*, 1969, and in *The Anno-
tated Lolita*, 1970.

4. The Poem   *The New Yorker*, June 10, 1944
Reprinted: *Poems*, 1959 and 1961;
Poesie, 1962, with Italian version

5. An Evening of Russian Poetry   *The New Yorker*, March 3, 1945
Reprinted as above; *Nabokov's
Congeries*, 1968, and in *The New
Yorker Book of Poems*, 1969

6. The Room   *The New Yorker*, May 13, 1950
Reprinted: *Poems*, 1959 and 1961;
Poesie, 1962, with Italian version,
and in *The New Yorker Book* of
Poems

7. *Voluptates tactionum*   *The New Yorker*, January 27,
1951
Reprinted as above

8. Restoration   *The New Yorker*, March 9, 1952
reprinted as above
and *Nabokov's Congeries*, 1968

9. The Poplar   *The New Yorker*, April 6, 1952
reprinted: *Poems*, 1959 and 1961
and *Poesie*, 1962